PREPARING THE *WAY* OF THE LORD

MIRIAM THERESE WINTER

ABINGDON
NASHVILLE

PREPARING THE WAY OF THE LORD

Copyright © 1978 by Medical Mission Sisters, Philadelphia, PA 19111

Library of Congress Cataloging in Publication Data

WINTER, MIRIAM THERESE.
  Preparing the way of the Lord.
  Includes bibliographical references.
  1.   Public worship.   I.   Title.
  BV25.W54   264'.02   78-7571

ISBN 0-687-33950-2

Scripture quotations in this publication unless otherwise noted are from
the Revised Standard Version Common Bible, copyrighted © 1973.

Scripture quotations noted JB are from The Jerusalem Bible, copyright ©
1966 by Darton, Longman & Todd, Ltd. and Doubleday & Company, Inc.
Used by permission of the publisher.

Scripture quotations noted Phillips are from the New Testament in
Modern English, copyright © J. B. Phillips 1958, 1960, 1972.

Scripture quotations noted TEV are from The Good News Bible: The Bible
in Today's English Version. Copyright © American Bible Society 1976.

The material on page 162 is from "Song of Liberation" by Miriam Therese
Winter. Copyright © 1978 by Medical Mission Sisters, Philadelphia,
Pennsylvania 19111.

Grateful acknowledgment to Management Design Incorporated (MDI) of
Cincinnati, Ohio, for basic leadership skills used in Part Two.

All songs in this book have been recorded by the Medical Mission Sisters
on various albums and are available from Avant Garde Records Inc., 250
W. 57th St., New York, NY 10019

MANUFACTURED BY THE PARTHENON PRESS AT
NASHVILLE, TENNESSEE, UNITED STATES OF AMERICA

To the One in whom we live and move and have our being, whose touch is a tongue of fire and whose love is my strength and my song, be glory and praise, honor and thanksgiving, forever and ever. Amen.

CONTENTS

PREFACE

Most people faced the effects of the modern liturgical movement without adequate preparation. We are still struggling to cope with consequences few really understand. There were many good reasons for changing established prayer patterns, but they were not widely known. Change progressed so rapidly that implementation outran efforts to educate in any systematic way. This left a large proportion of the faithful stunned, confused, threatened, or distrustful, forced once again to follow their leaders in blind obedience or to openly rebel. Not a very positive beginning to what would eventually make such an impact on so many lives. Thank God, those days are past.

In the years since that radical shift to contemporary styles of worship, much energy has gone into updating the people and dispelling alienation. Those pledged to implement change have paused in their forward motion to address the serious questions raised not only by the laity but also by those of the clergy who had been left uncomfortably behind.

These pages offer one more assist to that psychological transition. It is hoped that they might heal a few more wounds and lessen the gap still separating academic insight from its more practical application. What follows is a brief but serious glance at

purpose

11

contemporary corporate prayer. A loving look at history brings a traditional dimension to the trends of recent times. Page after page probes the relationship of God's living word to the way we live our lives. What does it mean? That is the question. What is the point of prayer?

This is a book for the people of God in parishes and congregations. It is addressed to laity and leaders together, gathered in churches or schools or religious communities for structured liturgy, mass, or service of worship, or in homes for a less formal prayer. It is intended for Protestants and Catholics, for those who have not yet attempted to introduce contemporary liturgical practice as well as those who have been a part of its ongoing reform. This book is designed for people who have something to gain from a deeper understanding of the facts of liturgical life as well as a lot to lose. Inhibitions, mainly. Rigidity. All the staunch stereotypes that cling to public prayer. Based on the belief that worship is not someone else's worry, this mini-course for congregations offers a piece of the action to those long sidelined on the benches. This course encourages not simply the stand-up, sit-down, sing-out motions, but serious participation in decision-making roles, encouraging even the uninitiated to make the most of their expertise.

Certain basic convictions have helped orient the direction of the text, namely, the patristic understanding of the liturgy as the work of the people of God and the importance of biblical theology in liturgical reconstruction. The latter has taught us that all knowledge, even biblical fact, is historically conditioned, that Scripture itself comes to us already

12

interpreted, shaped by particular points of view throughout its long and complex history of transmission. Consequently, we should be less fearful to take and make God's word our own. We are simply continuing the pattern of generations past. In our liturgical reenactment of God's historical interventions, we too seek contemporary meaning in mysteries that supersede understanding. This dalliance with transcendence is absurd to the unbeliever. But the person of faith knows that in the midst of a praying community one does indeed encounter the Holy, not only as memorial, but as event.

Explore God's word then, wisely and well, in the context of contemporary worship. Release its power so that it continues to be a *Heilsgeschichte* ("saving history") for us. Previous ages appropriated the record of God's saving deeds and embellished fact in the retelling. So we too tell and retell, relive as we remember, continue biblical tradition as we bridge past and present to transform and be transformed. As in the past, so now and into the future, God creates, liberates, redeems, and blesses in the terminology of the times. Liturgical prayer can and must relate this continuity, surprise us out of apathy, stretch us beyond ourselves. Scripture reveals its secrets to those gathered to confess its power, to the community that searches to shape itself according to biblical values. To these, revelation is always contemporary, Christ is always present, and recognized, in the breaking of bread.

This book is meant as a teaching aid to enable the average parish or congregation to take responsibility for prayer, both the design of it and the doing, with some degree of confidence. Many liturgical skills can be sharpened with effort and practice. You may have no resident "expert," but with sufficient motivation, you can do more than you realize. First admit that no one person has exclusive claim to the Spirit. Then begin where you are as a community, and build on what you have. Move forward gently, not so fast that you obliterate the value of the process. The point of prayer is not "getting there" but what happens on the way. Enough suggestions are included here to activate the imagination. The approach is to encourage you to contribute content of your own. Use the text as a handbook. Part One's rationale presents some background information. Part Two outlines a supportive framework for your creative thrust. Guidelines for getting started detail how to train local leaders to prepare the congregation to prepare and implement public prayer. For those already at ease with change, there are helps to deepen its meaning, to continue more creatively, to keep from going stale. Be sure to interpret the terms and the text from your own denominational standpoint. It is a challenge to address a book on corporate prayer to Christians across the board.

Liturgical reform extends an invitation to bring our behavior into line with religious principles and beliefs. Slowly, painfully, persistently, we are called upon to practice what we preach. Hear God's word and do it! That is the gospel mandate. Ritual that fails to stress this is worthless and insincere. The parable of the good Samaritan stands as a grim reminder: too often those committed to worship pass by on the other side.

Let me close by saying thank-you to all those large and small communities that caused this book to be—people throughout the United States and Canada, in Africa, Australia, Europe, Israel, Venezuela, New Zealand, and Fiji who welcomed both the context and the content of these ideas. Special thanks to McMaster Divinity College in Hamilton, Ontario, where much of this material took the shape of a course and where, in the midst of a supportive community, I was granted a degree; to the many families of Mennonites, Methodists, Baptists, Lutherans, Anglicans, Episcopalians, Presbyterians, Reformed, United Church, and Catholics, to all you dedicated Christians with whom I have lived, worked, studied, and prayed and felt so much at home. This book is the follow-up I promised you. You will recognize your presence here.

I am especially grateful to the Medical Mission Sisters, whose liturgical history is integral to my own life and spirit; to Anna Dengel, our foundress, who insisted on music although she did not sing a note; to Michael Mathis, C.S.C., who enticed us into the liturgical movement in its very early stages; to Loretta, Jane, and Mary Elizabeth for all that each has contributed to our ministry of word and song; to past and present members, in whose presence celebration happens and whose persons are rich resources for dynamic community prayer.

Basic concern = liturgical renewal of prayer - from a proper historical & practical base, with adequate instruction to enable all in this aspect of worship !

15

PART ONE

1

PRAYER AND THE PRAYING COMMUNITY

The explosion of liturgical insight and innovation characteristic of the past two decades marks yet another period of renewal for the church's public prayer. Before there was any hint of a structure, before formality supplanted spontaneous decisions to simply "come and see," one of the disciples said to Jesus: "Lord, teach us to pray" (Luke 11:1). Centuries have shaped and reshaped the context of our efforts. Our quest remains the same. Teach us how to pray! Through numerous reforms the real meaning of worship continues to elude us. Jesus reveals the dynamic of prayer bit by bit as his own life of prayer unfolds. He dwells on a quality of becoming, of knowing and being known. Even today our attention lingers on the level of structure and form. We are stung by his words to Philip because they fit us far too well. "Have I been with you all this time . . . and you still do not know me?" (John 14:9 JB).

Today we pour out our energies again in an effort to know the Lord. The current revitalization of worship has sent scholars back to early sources in search of some guidance through the maze of accretions collected through the years. It is painfully clear that the contemporary church has lost its early élan. We have forgotten what it feels like to burn

19

with tongues of fire. Our modern congregation bears little resemblance to the close-knit companionship of that community in the upper room. Our buildings are often empty, our services uninspired. A fair number among the faithful gather out of routine. It is hard to imagine that our modern fellowships emerged from that first following, where "the whole group of believers was united, heart and soul," where "everything they owned was held in common," where "none of their members was ever in want" (Acts 4:32-34 JB). We also long to gather gladly to praise the living Lord. We would preach with such conviction that again our membership would grow in numbers every single day. Current commitment to structure seems so far removed from the tone of the apostolic church. A crippling sense of emptiness leaves us desperately in want of roots. We seek a place like Lydia's house where all came together to encourage Silas and Paul. We are cursed with too much mobility. We are tired of leaving home. We would worship in a setting that does not restrict our struggle to become ourselves. How do we free the creative spirit imprisoned within lifeless forms? What does it mean to worship the Father "in spirit and in truth" (John 4:24 JB)?

The only worship acceptable today is a worship related to life, a worship that is of the people, a dynamic surge that forgives old griefs in a common pursuit of values: global awareness, a concern for justice, liberation long overdue. Such a worship springs from a basis of prayer, the prayer of a community comprised of praying persons who bring to the corporate experience a richness they choose to share. The vitality of worship depends on the vitality of personal prayer. The ritual problem is a prayer problem: so few of us really pray. A once-a-week-on-Sunday attitude kills corporate prayer. The church needs praying people—praying parishes, praying congregations, communities of praying persons. Lord, teach us how to pray!

The Praying Person

I learned to pray as a small child. I am sure you can say the same. I knelt at the side of my bed at night and chatted with an unseen God. It was all very important. I needed to give the whole list of those whom I would have God bless: the doll with the broken arm, the goldfish by the sink, Mommy, Dad, Grandma, Aunt Tess, and, on days of special fervor, that bratty kid next door. This kind of prayer was necessary. It made the whole thing real. Years passed. I grew older. The needs on my list changed. A generous God would surely get me a good mark on that exam. A just God would know I deserve a bike. Strength to meet my own expectations. Courage to cope with change. Though attitudes mature with the passing years, prayer patterns often stay the same. Prayer is a list for the benevolent Provider. It holds a hidden guarantee. A response toward my well-being means that God is really there. Then one day I encounter evil. In the hot blast of disbelief my house of cards comes down. I prayed, but God did not answer. Can faith survive the silence? Lord, teach me how to pray!

If we are serious at all about growing in grace, we must one day come to terms with the New Testament attitude toward prayer. We read, "pray continually" (Luke 18:1 JB), and its echo, "pray at all times" (I Thess. 5:17 TEV). How can we pray without ceasing when prayer is talking to God? Even those of us for whom words flow would find it tough to talk nonstop. Does that mean we are expected to fail? This traditional definition of prayer as conversation is still in vogue. Be on talking terms with the God-up-there. There is a God. Keep talking. When it is quiet, we are not so sure. There is a lot of talk in Scripture. Those casual conversations inspired our own approach to prayer. Adam, in the cool of the evening, walked and talked with God. Noah must have had some choice remarks about the notion of an ark. Look at the ease with which Abraham assumes the position of bargaining with God. He pleads that God spare Sodom for fifty, forty-five, thirty, twenty, even, he begs in desperation, for ten righteous men. God's word to Moses in the burning bush initiates a rapport. Plagues, laws, laxity, everything is discussed. God addressed Job from a whirlwind, having listened long enough. Some psalms are prayer-conversations. "How long, O Lord? Wilt thou forget me for ever?" (Ps. 13:1). The prophets converse with God. Fundamental to these conversations, however, is the fact that these people are God's friends.

Prayer is that relationship that grows with being friends. "I call you friends," said Jesus (John 15:15 JB). Friendship is how to pray. I "pray continually" when all that I do flows from a realization that God and I are friends. How exactly does this happen? One cannot program friendship. Usually the very pursuit of it makes everything go sour, but if one waits in readiness, one day, unexpectedly, friendship can occur. With God it can and does. New friends need to talk a lot, reveal to one another the puzzles that they are. They have to test what is happening. They have to be really sure. Each takes a turn at listening, shares perhaps unimportant things, asks a lot of questions, makes some small demands. This springtime of discovery is encouraging and affirming: we really get along! A beautiful time, beginnings, but the best is yet to come. Our relationship turns a corner when we realize a "we." We face the world together, experience life as "ours." This awareness does not happen all at once. It might take half a lifetime and more before intuition breaks through to insight and I experience: I know! I know I am not apart from God, do not journey as one at a distance, do not thirst as one deprived, but through God, with God, in God, love with an intense longing that envelops heart and will. Prayer then is the longing. Prayer is, in fact, the love. This love is Ground of Being from which words, deeds, inclinations spring, giving impetus and justification for all prayers prayed ever after. Such love is abiding presence, a presence transcending the physical plane as the absent One is always present to the one who really loves. Such love is an act of God in me that draws me out of myself. An awareness of being grabbed by God in whom "we live and move and have our being" (Acts 17:28) is what is meant by prayer. Some describe this as a hunger, others as a reaching out, an urgency to touch the intangible with the flesh his Flesh fulfilled. It is a whole new way of seeing. It is love making all things new.

What is true of any relationship applies equally to prayer. There is need for continual attentiveness to reactivate first fervor, to guard against going stale. A smile on Monday morning. A pause when I'm already late. A thank-you just because. Sometimes conversation. Sometimes just a word. Words. Deeds. Actions. Prayer is often activity, simply because so much of what we are is wrapped up in what we do. More important than all the doing is that time of being done. Time set aside for solitude, for slipping into a wilderness where love speaks to our heart. There are times in every relationship when the flow of words must cease, when we relinquish the "horizontal thinking" that prevents our "going down."[1] At the core of us, at the center, we are caught up beyond our capacity: the Lord is passing by! I saw you in the hurricane. Lord, in that earthquake, in that fire. You raise a lot of questions. Why so prone to tragedy? Why did they have to die? "Be still, and know that I am God" (Ps. 46:10). Be still and know. Be still. A "still small voice" reveals to the heart what the mind cannot understand. When all was in quiet silence, the "all-powerful word leaped from heaven . . . into the midst of the land" (I Kings 19:12; Wisd. of Sol. 18:14, 15) to lead me beside still waters, to comfort my troubled soul.

We are estranged from silence. It is alien to our times. We cover our tracks with racket, plug spaces with background noise. We talk or chatter endlessly to keep a stillness at bay. The stillness is too revealing. It peels away protective layers. It lets us touch transcendence. It tells us who we are. How elusive my own deep center. How narrowly my limits define. The Holy One, Designer of dust, made me as salt to be savored, as light to delight the world, made me image of that Image thrilling dry bones with a touch. Why then have I fled the Lord "down

24

the arches of the years"? Will he always follow after, whose utterance delineates my becoming, whose power gives strength to achieve? Alone in a solitude similar to those solitudes Jesus sought, I struggle for understanding, try to integrate Word and will. The stillness comes alive with feelings that the din of the day suppressed.

To pray means to wrestle these ghosts of God, to be stripped of choice priorities, to give myself away. "Batter my heart, three-personed God; for you as yet but knock," the poet in me prays. "Take me to you, imprison me, for I, except you enthrall me, never shall be free, nor ever chaste, except you ravish me."[2] Prayer is wrestling the stillness to the point of letting go, relinquishing past and future in trust of the enticing now. Prayer is being ready. Prayer is wasting time. We might ask ourselves, as friend of the Lord, when was the last time that I took time just to *be* with God, not with words or works or worship, but in the manner of being with someone I love, simply "wasting time"? When did I last slip beneath the surface to reach into my heart, shedding pressures, doubts, dailyness, to sit quietly at prayer? What of the cares that clamor for attention and confuse an attempt to pray? I do not know how to pray as I ought. I care too little. I care too much. Come, Spirit, come alive in me. You are the force that releases "in a way that could never be put into words" (Rom. 8:26 JB). You are the power of prayer in me. Touch my limits. Let my horizons expand. Be still! Forget about getting anywhere. Forget about trying or trying to forget. "Teach us to care and not to care. Teach us to sit still." Love, fear, doubt, confidence—the whole gamut of emotional paradox

25

accompanies a decisive experience of God. I am like the Rat in *The Wind in the Willows* when mystery overwhelms. "Are you afraid?" asks the Mole, as they are drawn like magnets to the Presence. "'Afraid?' murmured the Rat, his eyes shining with unutterable love. 'Afraid! Of Him? O never, never! And yet—and yet—O, Mole, I am afraid!'"[3] With this admission, the creatures bowed down and worshiped. With this admission, we creatures do the same.

An authentic renewal of the church's worship demands a genuine rebirth of prayer, a prayer that dares to lay claim on Presence, a prayer that begins within people who are in fact the church. We people of God must value prayer, strive with all our energy to know this Lord who came in person to reveal a personal God, a God who is relationship, the relationship of Father and Son whose Spirit is bond of love, relationship that spreads relationship across all boundaries of time and space. In our struggle to know this God, we must be careful not to fashion a god of our own designing by limiting our personal God to a person to whom we can relate. As friends, we must not cling to the Lord for the comfort of his flesh. Flesh, he says, does not define the One whom the whole world cannot contain, but hides a pledge of blessedness too splendid for the eye to see. In him, he says, we can approach the Other because he is for us the Way. Through him, he says, we can know the Father whom he represents. The more we come to know, it seems the less we know of God; yet faith insists that this is all we need to know to sustain a life of prayer. The key is recognition. We know: it is the Lord!

A reordering of priorities must follow recognition of the Lord. We value communication. We must value keeping still. We must move to restore that silence to which we have a right, protect parks and woods and empty spaces from the teeth of devouring cranes, secure some scope for solitude in the middle of the afternoon. There are 1,440 minutes in every busy day. We will not be praying persons if we cannot spend at least ten of those minutes quietly with God. We always find time for the things we love, for persons, hobbies, tasks. We can and we must find time for the stillness that strengthens the bond of prayer, that sharpens our perspective, that raises our consciousness to the fact that God is love, and love is here. Prayer then is a lifting up of the mind and heart to God, as that other definition says, just as long as we do not lift too high! For the God who is up is also beneath and around and behind and within. Prayer is a heightened awareness, in our minds and hearts, of God. It includes our conversations. It includes our sitting still. It shapes our going out to others and the sharing of ourselves. If this is what is meant by the mystical, then it is to be mystics that we are called.

Today we openly admit that contemplation is commonplace, not reserved for the rare individual busy about religious things, but a gift given to every one of us in varying degrees. This awareness of God, contemplation, goes by many names. I prefer to speak of a sabbath sense. Develop, cherish a sabbath rhythm, let it permeate the day, with time set aside for doing, with time just for being done. Don't wait until things get finished because you know they never do, but pause now and then in the flurry of

27

creating to reflect that it is good. A sabbath rhythm savors the Word that speaks all into being. In the spirit of Jewish sabbath, it restores a right relationship between ourselves, the world, and God. It sends us toward community determined to give our best, no matter what amount of turmoil tries to ravage inner peace. In the Quaker spirit it bids us speak when we have something to add to the silence, not like gongs or empty cymbals belching a babble of sounds. So ordered, let us now look further. Let us move into the worshiping community gathered together to pray.

The Praying Community

"Where two or more are gathered in my name, there am I in the midst of them" (Matt. 18:20). This collective act of a community of believers is commonly called worship. To worship, says the dictionary, is to pay honors to a deity by performing acts of adoration, veneration, homage, respect; by performing religious service. Worship is cultic activity. Until quite recently, the cultic expressions of most worshiping communities were somewhat stilted and remote, culled from a category of archaic actions reserved for God: a catalog of sacred gestures, a collection of sacred hymns, a specially designed service in a designated place. The word "worship" today seems to expect the word "service." The two together have connotations that are not easily dismissed. The phrase implies programmed action patterned on past experience that cannot, must not, change. Even in churches where there is no authorized ritual, the most binding of all codes

28

restricts ritual freedom: "We have always done it this way!" Worship, it would appear, is something that one does, or, as the dictionary puts it, performs. The service or liturgy is arranged and scheduled. It is an activity that we are expected to attend. Existing intact outside ourselves, it must meet our expectations, be acceptable to all.

How often have you heard on a Sunday morning after church: "What did you think of the worship?" or "How did you like the liturgy?" and "I didn't get anything out of it." People seem to perceive themselves as separate from their Sunday prayer experience when evaluating its impact. Ironically, many of us do want something to happen to us at worship, yet at the same time consider the worship to be more perfect when it is wholly other, untainted by the secularity that stamps our lives. A genuine renewal of worship demands that the "it" become an "us." This subtle shift of pronoun marks the pivotal point of change. What we are, what we do, what we offer, constitutes the worshiping community. It is we who praise the Lord. What we get depends on what we bring to the ritual. Enriched one hundred times over, our offering of love and commitment increases when linked to the richness in all. God's gift of self to us comes through our own giving which opens us up to receive. The strength of structural patterns must not overshadow corporate responsibility for energizing those patterns or even redesigning them, if need be, to elicit the people's prayer. Perhaps we might substitute the notion of "praying community" for that of "worship service" until we are convinced that it is people who make the structure work, that the sign of a valid structure is the fact that people

29

pray, that the focus of the problem or potentiality is within us. What we need today are not worshiping communities but praying communities that worship. This incarnational aspect strengthens the horizontal base from which our praise ascends, mingles a sense of the human with a sensitivity to the holy. We worship as community. We must therefore be a community, a community that really prays.

If our goal is a praying community, we have chosen no easy task. The two or more gathered in his name come to church as individuals, decidedly one by one. It is difficult to be a praying person; it is even more difficult to be a praying group. Individual prayer is a first step. Corporate prayer is more complex. In personal prayer we are free to develop our unique rhythm and style, find our own best way to God. No one way is better than any other. What is best is simply what works. Prayer patterns are linked to personal traits, to preferences and needs. There are many different personalities; there are as many different ways to pray. The crunch comes when many "free spirits" gather together for a collective prayer. The fact that all are praying persons does not necessarily ease the way, for what helps one may hinder another, what is right for one may be wrong for another, what is good for me may be devastating for you. Suppose I pray through modern music; you groove on classical chant. I like to sit; you prefer to stand . . . the list could go on and on. What is the solution when, week after week, we share a common pew? What makes a praying community? Obviously more than the sum of its praying persons. If personal prayer is relationship, then the clue to group prayer lies in an interrelationship that leads to a communal

awareness of God's presence within the group. Such
an awareness comes from and at the same time
creates an environment of attentiveness that underlies expressions of gratitude and praise. A community that shares a sense of Presence is a community
that prays. We have spoken a lot about praying. Let
us look at the concept of community, the qualifying
factor in corporate prayer, and see what we can
learn.

   What exactly is community? The term is not easy to
define. It covers a broad spectrum of possibilities—no two groups are quite the same—and carries
a load of nuances bestowed by an alienated
generation terrified of being alone. In any community, shared goals, dreams, or ideals create a
common bond. The intensity of that bondedness is
related to the dimension of choice. The choice can be
purpose or people, sometimes a bit of both. If I
choose in terms of a project, membership binds me to
all who join to participate in the task. The stress is not
on relationship. There is an external focus to which
all relate: a goal, a need, an ideology, a way to make a
living, some factor that binds participants together,
either loosely or in a tight, cohesive grip. Industrial,
political, educational organizations are structured on
this design. Membership bonds are by-products of
joint efforts to produce, manage, inform. Strangers
pull together. On medical teams and in military
maneuvers, the effort requires a high level of trust at
the risk of losing lives. Religious communities
resemble this pattern. Called by God to a life of
service, a candidate feels drawn toward teaching or
nursing, social work or contemplative prayer, in this
country or abroad. She chooses a religious order

31

involved in a particular ministry and blindly inherits those persons with whom she will spend her life.

It is similar within worshiping communities. The choice of denomination is mine. Other factors decide the rest. Territorial boundaries determine just which parish a Catholic will be in. Based on a concept of neighborhood, one is assigned to a parish, usually of enormous size, not according to what is preferred but according to where one lives. Even if I should choose to move into the territory of a particular parish, my co-parishioners are still not of my choosing. In Protestant churches you can worship where you like, provided that there is a church of your denominational choice nearby suited to meet your needs. Occasionally one chooses on the basis of a particular fellowship. More often one labors to form fellowship within the congregation of one's choice.

Some communities begin by choosing certain people who then establish goals: the family that grows from the marriage relationship, the bond between best friends, those small, spontaneous prayer groups, to a certain extent the house church, people preferring to be with particular people, working together for mutual good. Other groups form from a choice of persons thought to be compatible with an already envisioned goal. If I want to move a mountain, I don't begin with those who disagree. Some groups draw persons arbitrarily. Others pick and choose. These classifications are seldom clear-cut. There is emphasis one way or another, but usually an overlapping within.

The core community that gathered around Jesus was formed by his personal choice. He called. He selected. These few would join with him to inaugurate the mission he had in mind. They did not meet exclusively or close others out, even though their bond was special. Jesus was sensitive to all he met and had a much wider circle of friends. His warmth was felt by everyone, even the anonymous press of people who crowded around him time after time. He knew a variety of communities. His family in Nazareth, his friends in Bethany, each had its time and place. He broke bread for the multitudes, and at his final supper, he broke bread with those chosen few. Yet even from among his special disciples he selected several to share more intimately the mystery of his messianic role. These were part of the revelation on Mount Tabor and the anguish in Gethsemane when Jesus so desperately desired a community with whom he might wait and pray.

The Resurrection caused a radical change among those who were to form the nucleus of a church. The image of some ragtag followers around a charismatic leader shifted after their external focus was snatched away. Individuals became a cohesive group. The disciples continued to come together even after their leader was gone, at first simply for consolation in their grief and companionship in their fear. They met because in some undefinable sense they belonged to one another. They had been through so much together. Their lives were inseparably bound. They had known faith and faithlessness, felt all the fine pricks of learning how to love. They had followed a man, lived with him, loved him, and now they knew that he was indeed their long-awaited Lord. Prayer within such a group comes easily. We would imitate this model if we could. Awareness is keen. Love, belief, feelings are tightly integrated to a situation of gratitude and praise. Nevertheless, close-knit core groups such as this seldom last. Their bright, burning initiatives give impetus to movements that engulf them in their growth. To contain that uniqueness is to kill it, for maintenance and self-preservation focus inward while dynamism reaches out. That upper room was the nucleus of a movement determined to grow and spread. The group incorporated vast numbers, welcoming new members every day. Ironically, the building of the community was in a certain sense the start of its breaking down, moving Paul to stress the importance of building up the community emotionally and spiritually through elements in worship that would edify the membership and enrich the quality of its sharing. But more about that later.

What have we learned from all of this that applies to our here and now? Our church today follows the pattern of that apostolic community. We gladly welcome members, for the church is not an exclusive club but the vanguard of a driving force with good news for the world. Yet growth is the source of tension. People attach themselves to churches for various reasons, all of them very real. That early church was no bed of roses. Almost immediately there was a delineation of roles and procedures to provide for the many needs. Orphans, widows, the outcasts of society, the hungry, the impoverished, the secretive rich: many sought in the promise of a Kingdom instant liberation from present oppression. The community had to deal with all of this and with the disillusionment that followed when liberation was long in coming.

Each new member alters a group. This is one way that tension builds. Even today we bring to our church different ideas of prayer and quite different expectations of community. People come to church seeking some kind of community. The question is, how much? For some it is a matter of preference. For others it is an aching need. I come to church because I seek a larger gathering to which I can join my prayer. You might come craving friendship. You look to me for something more than I am prepared to give. I have other communities that fulfill my basic needs. I have my family and my friends. My church is where I pray. For another, the church is family. It might be all she has. Old, alone, and lonely, she lives out her week for Sunday, seeking from her worshiping community a deeper kind of bond. Our contemporary crucifixion is loneliness. Its reality overwhelms. It sells books, films, popular songs, and drives persons to clubs and to churches in an effort to escape its sting. The church perpetuates loneliness when it withholds relational bonds. Relationship follows on knowing, which precedes and follows love. But we are frightened of any self-revelation that might lead to our unveiling. So we gather in anonymity and cling to impersonal rituals to protect the secret that we are.

Ralph Keyes outlines the problem in his book *We, the Lonely People.* He writes: "A sense of community is what we find among people who know us, with whom we feel safe. That rarely includes the neighbors." [4] Or the congregation. Or the parish. We find it so difficult to entrust our feelings, especially to those with whom we share a bond, as if the revelation of our sheer humanity could somehow

35

cheapen our persons. Perhaps we are too much in love with the image of what we would be to trust the reality that we are. We prefer to worship side by side as acquaintances, or even strangers, successfully hiding the intensity of our feelings that might range all the way from hatred of change, to intolerance of certain people, to a love and appreciation that is seldom verbalized and therefore does little good. This is not a viable community. How then can our worship have dynamic force? We must take a long, hard look at the tone of our gathering before introducing patchwork attempts to revitalize our prayer. Are we satisfied to be, as Webster defines community, simply a body of people in the same place and under the same laws? Does joint owner-ship or participation, does common character or similarity define the community that we are or that we would want to be?

To the church of the twentieth century, lacking the security of tribal connections or the warmth of extended families, with its nuclear family falling apart, a definition based on law or geography is simply not enough. As Christians we may be thrown together arbitrarily, but there has got to be something more. And there can be. The bondedness of a caring community can be a source of grace, where joy shared is joy doubled and sorrow shared is sorrow halved, where the bearing of one another's burdens becomes the basis of shared prayer. Community for the Christian is more than adherence to a common creed or code. Community is a quality of relationship that communicates a sense of belonging transcending time and place. It is a deeply personal commitment universally shared, allowing me to be me and you to be you with all that this implies. Strengthened, this bond can and does strengthen, allowing from time to time moments of communion in the deepest sense of that word. Those created communities that are the churches must somehow struggle to create community in the manner outlined above. It will be worth the effort. Fringe people in our fellowships will know that they are wanted, empty lives will be awash with meaning, and the assembly will receive the energy it needs to formulate and to achieve its goals. If our church communities and our religious communities could resemble the team model in spots, duplicate that intense pursuit of purpose, that enthusiastic team-work, and those bonds that form in the process, imagine the impact on tired spirits. Each of our assemblies might attract a following equal to that of a football stadium on Sunday afternoon or a television audience on Monday night!

How can we sharpen our sense of sharing and see the building up of the community as a living commitment to prayer? We are limited in our choices. Common sense tells us that. Our congregation came into existence through a choice of the risen Christ, drawing together persons from many different walks of life. In this it resembles that apostolic community invited to follow the Lord. The disciples did not choose each other but, like us, were thrown together in response to a common call. It is encouraging to reflect that a feeling of togetherness could not have come easily to such an individualistic group. There were things that must have irritated: Peter's incessant bumbling, the extent of Judas' deceit, the arrogance of the Sons of Thunder, the fact that one among them was especially loved by Jesus. Before the events of Good Friday and Easter, all the sharp edges stand out. We are struck by the jealousy and the grumbling, the failures and the mistakes, the denials and apprehensions, the indignation when miracles occur through someone outside the fold. After Pentecost we see solidarity, a group. The disciples are no longer taken up with themselves. Pettiness, merely mundane concerns fade before the crisis of the Cross, the miracle of Resurrection, and the commission to spread the Word. There is meaning for us here.

Crisis brings people together. Projects do the same. Bonds develop among those who struggle to accomplish what they will to do. The more serious the undertaking, the more one commits oneself. The fight for social justice, in our neighborhood or the world at large, enables us to look outward together, forgetting our own small problems in the face of critical need. Any scrap of liberation achieved is an occasion to rejoice, and fellowship grows through the miracle of a worthwhile deed well done. Total choice may elude us, but a lot of choice remains. We can choose within the larger community to form small dynamic cells that give purpose and vitality to what could be an immovable mass. Prayer groups and study groups, teams concerned with community enrichment, and task forces formed for social action offer an alternative to anonymity and help build up the community into a community of friends. We need a circle of friends to come home to, a place where we know we are somebody and have something of significance to share, where we tap our gospel dimensions and discover that we are all pieces of a puzzling Word that speaks to our troublesome times. Some of us will walk on water. Some will wait at the foot of the cross. Some may spend the whole night fishing in vain. Some will fail to see the Lord. Some will be forgiven much because they have so much love. The task of a church that celebrates life is to welcome us as we are and to contribute to our becoming. The quality of that sharing matches the quality of its prayer.

This is easier to outline than to accomplish. We need more than goodwill to create community within the structured church. We need patience and compassion, a high tolerance threshold, and the facts of community life. It is a fact that much polarity stems from a radical or conservative bent. These tendencies influence our attitudes and how we act or react to change. By now we surely have some indication as to which way we are inclined. Do I thrive on variation or shun it? Did I applaud the liturgical changes, or would I have preferred to let things be? Am I radical or conservative? It is important that I know, because then I can anticipate my initial response and take time to think things through. To some, a radical is that pest who once took delight in reminding us that the God we adhered to was dead, one who is bound to be on the bandwagon of every passing fad. On the other hand, a radical perceives a conservative as one who is determined not to budge. The intensity of our particular point of view obviously colors our perception of truth. Each tendency has its good side that is too often overlooked.

We must shake loose from our pejorative images if we would learn from the past how to cope with further change before the pressure to adapt is upon us. For instance, consider what each contributes to the quality of life. Radicals intuit the future. They are our agents of change. A handful of dreamers who poke and probe and push ahead by challenging the status quo, they announce to the few who will listen and to the many who will not that the end of the world as we know it is very near at hand. Marginal people, ahead of their times, these early advocates of change drive others crazy with their innovative ideas. But their dreams are neither whim nor fancy. They cut through accumulated rhetoric with the razor edge of truth. Radicals do not treat tradition lightly as their critics would accuse. Their past is a precious heritage, a continuum of grace. They are radical, not in the revolutionary mode, but in that fundamental sense of having affinity for one's roots. They herald a return to sources. They insist on asking "why." Deeply concerned with values, they are convinced that systems must be sacrificed where meaning is at stake. Little by little their momentum builds until eventually the whole society moves ahead one giant step. By the time their notions become commonplace, however, radicals have already moved on. Change for the radical element is always too little and too late. They are fashioned for chasing rainbows, not for spending the pot of gold.

What of the conservative outlook that suffers every bit of the trauma that a cultural shift implies? Conservatives find any structural change terribly hard to take. They are the guardians of history. Their commitment to style and practice means that they are likely to cherish every ritual as a treasure to be preserved. How a thing is done is just as important

40

as why it is done at all. Their love for the trappings of tradition offers stability to a world in flux. They would guarantee forever the keepsakes of the past: turkey every Thanksgiving, no Christmas without a tree. They are not the sponsors of progress; they collect its souvenirs. In a congregation or parish or religious community, some members are radical while others are conservative to the core. Most, however, fall somewhere between the two extremes, leaning to one side or the other to set an overall tone.

If we want a praying community, it is important to know and appreciate precisely where each member stands, for our basic orientations affect our plans and projects and prayer. First we must confront faulty assumptions and talk about how we feel, resisting the temptation to label people and put them in a box. Accept that I am a dreamer, that you are pragmatically inclined. I know my idea is going to work even if I cannot tell you how. You know it won't without a lot of effort, and you would rather not be involved. I cringe if I am continually corrected back to some unseen norm. You can't see why I am always doing something that will break the rules. I know that you are cautious, but I relish taking risks. A first step forward in cementing fellowship is to find out how people feel. A real breakthrough comes with the discovery that we are not out to massacre each other's values or to be ugly or stubborn or flip but that we respond a certain way simply because that is the way we are. Sensitivity to one another's feelings can ease aggravation into tolerance, into appreciation, into love. Once we accept that we are different we can begin to feel as one, sharing our gifts and talents instead of treating them as threats.

41

Some tensions in community will never be completely erased. These rise from our basic differences and surface in community prayer. Simply said, they concern an orientation toward freedom of spirit or law. There are two attitudes toward worship. One is the call of the Spirit to spontaneity and freedom, the other a call through formality to a structured, systematic prayer. One is the way of Abraham. The other is the way of Aaron.[5] Both are legitimate approaches because both ways are of God. So compelling is an adherence to one or the other that often individuals transcend denominational differences to find fellowship among those who feel similarly drawn. Like Abraham, some of us hear God's call to come out of our complacency and leave all security behind, following in faith an uncharted course, confident that God will guide us. As enticing as the Abrahamic way might seem to all those tired of too much structure, it is important to remember that it was God who enjoined upon Aaron and his descendants the minutiae of rituals and rules. There is mystery here and a level of meaning that evades our understanding. Indeed, this seems to be one of the critical questions of our times, the validity of structure on the one hand, the legitimacy of ad hoc worship on the other.

Congregations of the future may form around a preference for either way, but for most of our parishes and congregations today, it would seem that our worship must lie somewhere in a balance between the two, between unlimited freedom and unquestioning conformity, between spontaneity and restraint. The delicacy of discerning how much of each makes a viable mix must surely be left to the

Spirit who informs the praying community. Perhaps for now it is best to add some freedom to our structures by incorporating individual gifts. Our gifts can enrich our ritual as we aim for a balance more meaningful than compromise, worshiping in a variety of styles so that now and then each member of the community can feel at home. There is freedom and growth in diversity when we are big enough to bend a little to incorporate some gesture, some song, some action that another member loves. Continuity comes with the ongoing love that we have for one another. Embrace and bless individuality. Do not be frightened when it begins to stretch our narrow and limited lives. Do not be discouraged if it seems that our worship is a continual tug of war. Authentic worship is related to life, and life is full of tension. If our worship does not reflect some tension, our prayer will not be real.

Let us pause to sum up the preceding pages before moving on. This reflection on prayer and the praying community is not a how-to manual. It is more along the lines of a rationale, leaving space between the lines for each reader to fill in a personal program of do's and don'ts. Our concern has been the quality of worship. We have seen how we wrongly attribute to ritual those problems of a social sort: a lack of understanding, a lack of communication, tensions underlying a loosely knit group that deals far too superficially with the vital facts of life. Tensions of just plain living hover over our attempts to pray. We seesaw precariously between the already and the not yet as legalists set conditions and lobbyists shatter norms. Some new groups today begin and build together form a common philosophical base, but that

43

describes precious few. Most communities continue to evolve in terms of their own histories, often reactionary and riddled with pain. The important thing now is that each community reflect upon itself, name its problems and its potential and accept these for what they are, then proceed to clarify directions by setting achievable goals. Under good, enabling leadership, a concerned community can delineate roles and expect shared responsibility for its worship and its works. A lot will be learned in the process. Often the process itself will be as important as the result, for the struggle to achieve consensus builds up both community and commitment, setting a tone that ensures success because no one is left out.

A praying community is in touch with itself, with the world at large, with God. This is in fact its worship, reaching up and out and in. The dynamism of praying persons will attract other praying persons that were once driven from the structured church by restricting, impersonal forms. After years of trial and error in convents and rectories and churches, we are convinced that praying together does not automatically create community in the sense of relational bonds, but rather it affirms, enriches, and deepens those bonds that already exist. Fellowship bonds are by-products of honesty together, initiated outside of structured worship and celebrated within. It is good therefore to be doing together, but pardon a cautionary word. If we are busy about too many things, however necessary, there may be little time or desire or energy to pray. Cling to the notion of sabbath. See that it is shared by all. It is good just being together in the presence of the Lord, a rest stop on the road of life where, huddled against exhaustion and the fury of constant storms, we gain strength from some bread, some wine, some sharing: a bit of fellowship on the long, long journey through darkness into light.

Authentic worship comes from a praying community; a praying community needs praying persons; a person prays, a group prays, when it recognizes the Lord. If we turn to the Gospels for guidance, we will be startled to discover that we can find no model there. The disciples first followed Jesus without knowing he was the Lord, and there is no indication during that whole time spent with Jesus that they prayed together as a community. As Jews they went to synagogue and observed the traditional feasts, but they had no uniquely Christian worship in the sense we have described. Once it was mentioned to Jesus about John and his disciples, how they were always offering prayers. The answer Jesus gave is the key to Christian prayer: "The days will come, when the bridegroom is taken away . . . and then . . ." (Luke 5:35).

During those years that Jesus spent with his disciples, he talked a lot about prayer, taught them how to pray, often went off by himself to pray, even prayed to the Father for all of them. But they did not pray together. The Last Supper was to be the Passover observance until Jesus made it something more. Other opportunities failed miserably. The response to Tabor was, build a shrine! In the Garden of Olives, on the brink of death, those who gathered fell asleep. The time had not yet come. Only after Jesus had gone away and his followers realized who he was did they gather and "with one accord devoted themselves to prayer" (Acts 1:14). Surely the message here is that of a new order of prayer. The time had come for a praying community, for entering into that relationship with Father, Son, and Spirit, for gathering in the name of Jesus and affirming him as Lord. Christian prayer is God made present after God-made-man is gone. Prayer is presence in absence, the activity of the Spirit that links us to our God. The prayer of a praying community is knowing what the Word really means and daring to say: our Father!

2

LIVING WORD,
BREAD OF LIFE

I tell you most solemnly, whoever listens to my
words, and believes in the one who sent me, has
eternal life. . . . I am the bread of life . . . who comes
to me will never be hungry . . . who believes in me
will never thirst. . . . The words I have spoken to you
are spirit and they are life.

(John 5:24; 6:35, 63 JB)

As the disciples lifted their eyes to their ascending
Lord, a miracle slipped between their fingers ending,
with awesome finality, that first in-the-flesh introduction to faith. When they looked again to earth, the
only terrain they knew, they saw a new order of
being, life and all its processes irrevocably linked to
its life-giving source. How little they actually knew of
the man they had left all to follow. So much of what
their friend had shared with such urgency and
insistence had escaped them. Bread, Kingdom, his
presence in their midst—all had been received in a
literal sense. Now that the wrench of departure had
torn away the veil, every facet of his life among them
was examined under the penetrating focus of their
love. So began the long, laborious process of
remembering that is the mark of Christian contemplation. They relished recalling events that had such
power to fill the hollows of their hearts, savored

47

words that seemed to satisfy a craving for continuity. Those who once wondered what it meant to pray, reflected and prayed.

In his book *The Birth of the New Testament,* C. F. D. Moule suggests that much of what we now know about the New Testament we owe to early Christian worship, where the words and deeds of Jesus were recalled, preserved, and transmitted to succeeding generations.[1] In the setting of worship, Jews and Gentiles, eyewitnesses and those who believed without seeing, all who claimed allegiance to Christ could encounter firsthand the Lord of history as living Word and bread of life. In the setting of worship, snatch phrases were transformed into maxims revealing that the life and death of one man was for the salvation of all. Once insight shattered the shell encapsulating understanding, the apostles set out eager to tell of all they had seen and heard and experienced and were only beginning to comprehend. They returned to pray together daily, gathering in and around that Word as source and summit, wellspring and harvest, inspiration and motivation, for all who felt compelled to perpetuate the name.

There is something to be gained from a backward glance at the rudiments of Christian worship. We might see reflected in that mirror image, however darkly, a flash of form uncluttered with elaborate ritual dress as well as attitudes to match our own. There is no going back to past simplicities, not in any physical sense. Nicodemus understood that when he quipped about an inability to return again to his mother's womb. But we can strip away useless frills and gaudy encumbrances to tap into fundamental strengths, as a spiral returns to its starting point but always on a different plane, deeper or higher than before. In that sense we can indeed be born again through a rediscovery of values that have held down through the centuries. Those fundamentals of Christian worship can help us evaluate the implications of evolving practice and guide our design of suitable supportive structures that will enable basics to be meaningful today.

Recall
of Xn
worship
background

Christian worship emerged from a Jewish context. The disciples continued to attend the synagogue and the Temple just as they always had, until their acknowledged adherence to the Lord Jesus became incompatible with their allegiance to Judaism, and they either left or were thrown out of the Jewish minyan. The book of Acts verifies both the Jewish and the Christian aspects of early worship, stating that the first Christians "went as a body to the Temple every day but met in their houses for the breaking of bread" (Acts 2:46 JB), and "they preached every day both in the Temple and in private houses" (5:42 JB). The Christian church began as a house church, meeting in "the upper room where they were staying" (1:13 JB) and then in the homes of the members: the house of Mary, mother of John Mark, "where many were gathered together and were praying" (12:12) and, as we note from greetings sent, in houses throughout the Diaspora: "greet Prisca and Aquila . . . greet also the church in their house" (Rom. 16:3-5); "greetings to the brethren at Laodicea, and to Nympha and the church in her house" (Col. 4:15); "to Philemon . . . and Apphia . . . and Archippus . . . and the church in your house" (Philem. 2). The initial gatherings took place daily and then on a weekly basis, "on the first day of the week" (Acts 20:7). "On the day called after the sun, a meeting of all who live in cities or in the country takes place at a common spot."[2] So arose the notion of a Christian sabbath, a special Easter celebration once a week on Sunday, the Lord's Day (see Rev. 1:10; Didache 14:1).

There were three distinct phases in the history of early Christian worship. The first was the eyewitness period. Brief, vivid, optimistic, the tone of worship was dominated by those who had actually seen the Lord. The remembering was not a cerebral recollection, but a dynamic reliving of past events, as veterans relive the foxhole camaraderie of long-forgotten wars, as a family is rejuvenated recalling milestones of its past. In such situations, to remember is to make real again. There is no need for structure. Love initiates and forges a deep-feeling bond, because everyone has already participated in some way in the reality recalled.

Shortly after Pentecost, the power of Peter's preaching added to their number a crowd of significant size. Soon eyewitnesses were outnumbered by those who had neither seen nor heard the Lord but had experienced vicariously, by hearsay, what others knew firsthand. This second phase was characterized by a concern for saving every shred of information that might be handed on. It marked the growth of an oral tradition. Each community had its favorite parables and sayings to keep. As the gap between the Resurrection and its recollection increased, some realized that time might eventually cloud the clarity of recall or embellish the facts as so often happens when one is handed a piece of good news and told to pass it on.

This led to a third phase, that of recorded history, when the Christ story was chronicled so that future believers might learn from books the content of the faith. We live in this latter time of insight through Inspiration that reaches back into that first century after Christ. It is to this period that we trace many of the elements used in worship today. We are closer to our roots than we might imagine. Cultic expressions change with the changing times. Some practices were eliminated and eventually rediscovered, others were added and then removed under pressure of liturgical reform. An authentic return to sources does not mean worshiping now as they worshiped then, but it means experiencing now a similar enthusiasm for the faith. A contemporary expression of traditional values is the key to a genuine renewal of spirit.

Little is actually known of early church practice because literature is lacking and references to worship are scarce. Sources until the year A.D. 150 include the New Testament Acts of the Apostles; the Epistles, particularly Paul's to the church at Corinth; the book of Revelation; and several nonscriptural writings: a letter from Clement, Bishop of Rome, to Corinth; some lines from Pliny's letter to the emperor; a passage from the First Apology of Justin Martyr; and a chronicle of early liturgical practices in a document known as the Didache. These indicate that tradition quickly took shape around three basic practices: preaching, prayers, and the breaking of bread. Today, after centuries of shifting standpoints and cultural change, we too have remained faithful "to the apostle's teaching and fellowship, to the breaking of bread and the prayers" (Acts 2:42).

As soon as the coming of the Spirit had loosened

their tongues and freed their imprisoned spirits, the apostles went out and preached with an intensity that knew no bounds. The Acts of the Apostles seems to substantiate its claim that "their proclamation of the Good News of Christ Jesus was never interrupted" (Acts 5:42 JB). From the beginning there was an urgency to connect the life and words of Jesus with the whole of salvation history showing how, from earliest times, the coming of Jesus as Messiah and Lord was foreordained and that in him elemental expectations were fulfilled. Preachers were jeered and jailed for their commitment to spreading the news. Stephen in effect preached his own eulogy when he told how, in times past, they killed those who foretold the coming of the Just One. Those who escaped persecution endured continual harassment, and the courage of their convictions brought multitudes into the church. A thorough knowledge of Scripture, the hallmark of a Jewish heritage, enabled a convincing application of past prophecies to present events. Time and time again, preachers addressed Christians as "heirs of the covenant God made with our ancestors" (3:25 JB), pointing out that "it was this salvation that the prophets were looking and searching so hard for; their prophecies were about the grace which was to come to you" (I Pet. 1:10 JB). In addition to evangelization, early preaching had another important purpose, one directed toward the edification of the community of believers. All those who had been informed had then to be instructed, those who heard the Word and believed had always to be inspired. Apprentices in the faith were taught their responsibilities and made aware of all that fidelity implied.

Full-fledged members sought inspiration and strength. Like newborn babies they had tasted a new creation and now hungered for a total transformation of life. Sermons helped them integrate the Word as a way of life.

The first corporate act of the new sect, the selection of Matthias to replace Judas the traitor, occurred in the context of shared prayer (Acts 1:23-26). Early Christians must have lived in an attitude of prayer, for prayer is, quite simply, remembering. The event had been so recent, the experience of conversion so total, the assent to faith so dangerous, surely they contemplated the force that had altered their lives so radically. Paul suggests this probability when he writes: "Whatever is true, . . . whatever is just, whatever is pure, whatever is lovely, whatever is gracious, if there is any excellence, if there is anything worthy of praise, think about these things" (Phil. 4:8). In addition to a climate of prayer, there were specific prayers shared during times of worship. Some were patterned prayers repeated at community gatherings. Others were freely composed on the spot by the prophetic voices in their midst. The Didache points out that "the prophets may give thanks as much as they want" (Did. 10:6), and Paul makes frequent reference to the validity of prophetic prayer in his discourse on tongues (I Cor. 14).

The Lord's Prayer seems to have been said liturgically from earliest times. The reminder in Romans 8:15 that as God's children we are able to cry out "Abba, Father!" indicates an ease with addressing God in the manner taught by Jesus. Chapter 8 of the Didache directs Christians to pray the Lord's

Prayer three times daily, and adds to the scriptural text the doxology, "for thine is the power and glory forever." This doxology, or "Protestant ending," to the Lord's Prayer has been the cause of more ecumenical confusion than one might imagine and has hung like a declaration of war between Protestants and Catholics since the Reformation. It is in fact neither scriptural nor Protestant, but simply a liturgical response to the words of the Lord, an extended congregational Amen, so to speak, to the prayer prayed by Jesus and now shared by us all. Its appearance in the Didache is evidence that this ending was already in use in the apostolic church. Catholic liturgical reform of the sixties added this doxology to the Lord's Prayer at Mass, separating Catholics and Protestants now by only a few short sentences that were inserted between. The Lord's Prayer invites us to stand in the place of Jesus and address God as Father. In this sense it is Christian, yet it can be prayed comfortably by all of God's children as they look to their Creator to meet their needs.

The oldest specifically Christian prayer is the Maranatha, or "Come, Lord Jesus!"—the final phrase in the New Testament (Rev. 22:20). It has been handed down in its original Aramaic form, attesting to its age and to the possibility that the phrase was similar to a motto or slogan and enjoyed widespread use. The prayer addresses Jesus as Lord, a posture distinctly Christian, and looks to him to vindicate the just, liberate the enslaved, and fulfill the promises of glory and peace. The tenth chapter of the Didache places it in a liturgical context: "Let grace come and let this world pass away, 'Hosanna to the God of

54

David.' If anyone is Holy, let him come; if anyone is not, let him repent, Maranatha. Amen." This short phrase was and still is a profoundly Eucharistic prayer, addressing the Person whose presence is expected. It was the cry of a disenfranchised sect, cast out by the Jews, suspect by the Gentiles, yet convinced to the point of martyrdom that vindication would surely come. Despite growing threats of persecution and the increasing incidence of violence that surrounded their proclamation of the Word, Christians dared affirm Jesus as Lord, calling on him to come again, now, to strengthen and encourage their fragile faith, quickly, with the promise of deliverance and the splendor of everlasting life.

The first Christians met together regularly at mealtime. This custom was a daily reminder of that final supper with the Lord, when he broke bread with them and told them to perpetuate the practice in his memory. It was also a reminder of his appearances to them at mealtimes after the Resurrection, when he revealed himself to the disciples in Emmaus as he sat with them at table and broke bread (Luke 24:30), when he sought out the eleven astounded apostles and their associates, dispelling their disbelief by eating some grilled fish (vv. 42:43), when he joined them all at the edge of the lake for breakfast (John 21:12). So in a setting of food and fellowship, they met to remember and rejoice, convinced that he would be with them again as they preached, prayed, and participated together in that solemn ritual act, the breaking of bread. Their Maranatha recalled his previous presence at meals and called upon him to come again in the Spirit he promised would fill that little while between his comings, as they awaited in faith and fellowship, in communion with him and with each other, that final messianic feast foreshadowed in the parables of the wedding banquet (Matt. 22) and wedding feast (25) and foretold at the Last Supper (26:29).

The meal was an important symbol in the early church. It signified that threefold presence: in the past, here and now, and in fullness at the end of time. Eating with Christ was a sign of election and commissioning: "God raised him on the third day and made him manifest; not to all the people but to us who were chosen by God as witnesses, who ate and drank with him after he rose from the dead" (Acts 10:40-41). The tragedy of the Cross faded before the miracle of Resurrection, and a sense of presence overshadowed an initial sense of loss. They came together gladly (2:46), in a framework of celebration, with festive spirits and happy hearts. In time, that agape atmosphere deteriorated, at least in Corinth, where the community seemed to miss the entire point of the common meal. Paul had to chide them for their obnoxious behavior, reminding them that the impetus for assembling was, after all, the death of the Lord Jesus and that wanton revelry had no place among Christians pledged to care for one another (I Cor. 11:17-34). Still the concept of an actual meal continued until, for whatever reason, it evolved to a ritual meal. This was the case by about A.D. 150 as is evidenced in a passage from Justin. In succeeding centuries it evolved even further, from a ritual meal to a ritual that emphasized more and more the notion of Christ's death and our salvation through the sacrifice of his blood on the cross.

A whole theology of sacrifice developed along

with the evolution of a priesthood, and the liturgical reenactment of the Last Supper shifted its emphasis from celebration to oblation. The table became an altar, the meal became an offering, the Lord was hailed as Saving Victim, participation and shared fellowship succumbed to the stress on mystery, and Christians became silent spectators at a sacred action performed by special ministers in a ceremonial way. From meal to ritual meal to ritual sacrifice, and a distinct theology of presence, that focused more and more on the elements of bread and wine and less and less on the community gathered together to break bread. The pre-Pauline approach to Eucharist, before his attempt to correct Corinth back to a norm sowed seeds for a shift in stress, that sense of celebration evident in the Didache has found renewed emphasis in our times. Perhaps we can recapture too that sense of community as we welcome our risen Lord into the midst of our assembly.

By the time Justin writes (approximately A.D. 150), Christian worship has acquired a distinct shape. In essence it is similar to our contemporary service. Its two-part structure corresponds to the Liturgy of the Word/Liturgy of the Eucharist design of a contemporary mass and to a typical Protestant Eucharist of various denominations. The gathering no longer takes place within the framework of a meal. The breaking of bread is a ritual act. Elements of worship with which we are familiar are already part of the tradition.

On the day after the sun a meeting of all who live in cities or in the country takes place at a common spot and the Memoirs of the Apostles or the writings of the Prophets are read as long as time allows. When the reader is finished the leader delivers an address through which he exhorts and requires them to follow noble teachings and examples. Then we all rise and send heavenwards prayers. And, as said before, as soon as we are finished praying, bread and wine mixed with water are laid down and the leader too prays and gives thanks, as powerfully as he can, and the people join in, in saying the "Amen"; and now comes the distribution to each and the common meal on the gifts that have been brought.[3]

Instead of a meal at which the Word is shared, there is a service in which the proclamation of the Word is followed by the Eucharist, the ritual breaking of bread. Today Protestants recognize two separate services, a service of the Word which is normative for most and the less frequent Eucharist service in the manner described above. Catholics continue to celebrate two aspects of one liturgical act.

There are some definite statements as well as numerous hints about early liturgical practice in the literary sources we have on hand. The earliest confession of faith was the simple and enthusiastic affirmation: Jesus is Lord! This sufficed for a creed, for it proclaimed belief in the death, resurrection, and glorification of Jesus the Christ. Reconciliation was an important prerequisite to the breaking of bread. The Didache and Paul echo the gospel injunction (Matt. 5:23-24): if anyone has a quarrel with another, he or she must first be reconciled before approaching the table of the Lord. There are also references to a greeting: "Greet one another with a holy kiss" (Rom. 16:16). With such a stress on reconciliation, it would seem that this greeting was an important ritual gesture, assuring forgiveness and cementing the bond of fellowship and love.

58

Paul begins his letters with what may have been the traditional greeting at the start of worship and ends them with what could be the transition formula from the shared Word session to the breaking of bread. These stylized liturgical formulas suggest that Paul's letters were read to the community assembled for worship. Certainly some were. Now and then Paul insisted on a public hearing. "I adjure you by the Lord that this letter be read to all" (I Thess. 5:27). It is uncertain just when the reading of Scripture was added to the shared remembering of the words and deeds of Jesus. Perhaps right from the beginning. The Old Testament Law and the Prophets would, of course, have been the only recorded Scripture available to the primitive church.

Other elements of early Christian worship include the congregational Amen. This carried over from the Jewish liturgy and continued as the people's response. The psalms, hymns, and inspired songs will be discussed later on. Little is known about free expressions of the Spirit, such as revelation or prophecy, which was an inspirational sharing, speaking in tongues, and the interpretation of tongues. These charismatic gifts disappeared fairly early from formal worship under stress for clarity, coherence, and comprehension regarding any contribution to corporate prayer. Finally, it is important to realize that not every Christian community worshiped in precisely the same way. The church of Jerusalem was bound to differ from the churches of the Gentiles. The style that flourished at Ephesus was definitely not the approach of Rome.

Some two thousand years after that first Pentecost and the birth of what we now call church, Christians continue to gather on the Lord's Day in myriad communities around the world. Some still meet in homes in an environment of spontaneous worship, most collect in spaces especially set aside for the formal reenactment of a service whose outline could be dimly perceived during the decades after Christ. Our looking back at what was has had a definite purpose: that our rediscovery of root values might spur us on to take a serious and loving look at what our worship is now and what it could be in the years ahead. Our view of history is somewhat distorted because we have seldom taken time or opportunity to learn how our worship practices began and why. Early liturgical practice had a reason. It was aimed at building up the community. Whatever elements were incorporated into the worship experience, whether instruction, prayers, songs, or expressions of reconciliation and belief, were for the edification of the membership. Faced with discrimination and threats of persecution, much stress was placed on strong bonds of fellowship and a deepening of faith. Whatever did not contribute to this mutual strengthening and inspiration had no place in the worship setting. Paul makes this clear to the community at Corinth, subjecting the prophetic and charismatic gifts to severe scrutiny in order to test their validity in communal prayer (I Cor. 14). That gathering in a spirit of thanksgiving and praise, that day-by-day and then week-by-week doing of worship, was primarily to help the group. We tend to forget this, we who do rites of worship for God. We forget to do something for us. If our worship would be truly a *beracah,* a grateful blessing of the Creator who makes all things new, it must be a sensitive, refreshing, renewing statement to us. We sing and pray and listen and reflect in order that we might be connected to the Source and Summit who is life in and around us. We come together that we might inspire and be inspired, renew and be renewed, encourage and be encouraged, affirm and be affirmed in faith, in hope, in love.

What seems characteristic of those early gatherings to build up the body of the church is a comfortable balance between what Oscar Cullmann calls free expression and fixed liturgical form. A certain patterned regularity emerges with ease. There is a coming together for food, both physical and spiritual, and for remembering with meaning. The shape is loose yet definite. The content is fairly free. There is no prescribed order in which the elements must occur. What is preached, who prays and how, what is sung and shared, these vary. The notion of reconciliation and the holy kiss added a touchingly human dimension to every meeting of the group. Daily worship was never routine, because corporate prayer was close to the dynamic ebb and flow of life. How the skeptical world was treating the believers was surely a subject of sharing as each member sought strength and assurance and some kind of guidance to face another difficult day. Since adherence to Christianity at that time often split families, led to social shunning, and forced some members to live secret lives, communal worship was an opportunity to gather with like-minded people and say collectively that it was worth it.

Strikingly absent from early literature is any insistence on roles within worship. Paul speaks instead of gifts. His discourse on "varieties of gifts, but the same Spirit" (I Cor. 12:4) interrupts his instruction on Eucharist and the proper behavior at worship. "To each is given the manifestation of the Spirit for the common good," says Paul (v. 7). Then he lists the various kinds of gifts given to individuals, so that through the Spirit's inspiration each one might contribute toward the building up of the body which is the church. The placement of this passage implies that Christians participated freely in worship according to individual inclination, some contributing extemporaneous prayer, others sharing an inspirational reflection. And if there is any doubt, Paul specifically writes: "When you come together, each one has a hymn, a lesson, a revelation, a tongue, or an interpretation. Let all things be done for edification" (14:26). There is a tone of trust and sharing, an appreciation of God's gift in every person, a sense of building on one another's insights. "Let two or three prophets speak, and let the others weigh what is said. If a revelation is made to another sitting by, let the first be silent. For you can all prophesy one by one, so that all may learn and all be encouraged; and the spirits of prophets are subject to prophets. For God is not a God of confusion but of peace" (vv. 29-33).

The leadership of early worship differed from the priestly profile we so easily assume. Most likely the leader coordinated the service, initiated the breaking of bread, and enabled individual participation, encouraging whatever might build up the body through edification and inspiration, discouraging whatever might disturb or confuse the group. In time the leader or elder or presbyter acquired more ritual responsibility, eventually performing the functions

62

of a hierarchical priesthood patterned after the priestly tradition of Judaism. But that was later on. In the beginning, liberty and continuity blend to create a beautifully balanced worship. In his book *Early Christian Worship,* Oscar Cullmann sums up the situation with some implications for us.

It is precisely in this harmonious combination of freedom and restriction that there lies the greatness and uniqueness of the early Christian service of worship. With this high aim of the "building up" of the community, of the body of Christ, constantly in view, Paul does not fall into the error of reducing the worship life of the Church to a minimum from fear of the binding character of liturgy, nor yet does he, out of fear of sectarianism, fall into the error of eliminating on principle from the service of worship all free expressions of the Spirit. Had it been possible to maintain this harmony in the service of worship the formation of sects and groups would have been most effectively checked.[4]

Twentieth-century liturgical reform is characterized by a search for a fundamental faith expresssion appropriate for today. Today we have no patience with what seems superfluous or unreal. The worshiping church, locked into a rigidity of its own choosing, is struggling to shake loose from irrelevant restraints. It is a tough undertaking. What begins with the head must be embraced by the heart, and it takes time for understanding to seep through the system. The church is sore all over, for if even one member suffers, the whole body aches. One does not simply negate feelings, deny inhibitions, pick up the pieces of one's broken myth, and move merrily on. Each historical period honed liturgical structures to meet situations, real or imagined, to which the church saw fit to react. Consequently we who inherit that history find we have been reared in a reactionary framework. The church that once welcomed what its members had to offer did a complete turnabout and fought vehemently to keep personal expression out. Today the church's challenge is to restore that delicate balance between impromptu and patterned prayer. The most precious insight of this age of the Spirit is the rediscovery that as people we are all of a piece—body and soul, material and spiritual, secular and sacred—that a wholehearted response to the gospel demands a whole-person, wholly human response. We people of God-made-flesh struggle now to reintroduce wholeness into our ritual so that we might

overcome the strange and unhappy paradox that in practice the religion of the Incarnation has not realized its own essential meaning—the wedding of the flesh to the spirit. Instead of effecting the union of God and the world, which is its central purpose, Christian sacramentalism has kept the two apart.[5]

If worship is to express the life of a people in a wholly human way, then people must share the responsibility for worship and participate not only in its actualization but also in its preparation. Only those involved in the living can guarantee a harmony between an expression of life and an expression of belief. Participation in a shared responsibility for worship presumes some notion of what the worship experience is all about and what might be suitable components to achieve the desired end. Worship, we have noted, is a coming together in gratitude and praise to feel the reality of God in order to sharpen our sensitivity to what God's will demands of us. There are times when the experience just happens, when a group simply collects and, with little or no preparation, is immediately caught up in a genuine fellowship of praise. This is common in small groups such as house churches, where members are well known to one another and are immediately in touch as a group. More often worship requires effort, preparation, work, if it would be more than lip service or a rote repetition of rites. It takes grace and skill to weave together life's raw materials in relation to God's word after the manner of Jesus. If we look to the Lord for a model, we note his concern for environment, his free use of all of creation in the preaching of his word, and his keen sense of presence, his own and that of his Father.

Jesus cared about the environment within which he proclaimed his message, the environment in which he prayed. He selected his setting for solitude, going off into the desert or up into the mountains to pray. He also carefully arranged the setting for his service of the word. He went up to Jerusalem, into the synagogue, climbed into a boat and pushed off from the shore, settled the crowds on a grassy hillside, entered a house, sat at table, paused before a tomb, walked on water, wrote in the sand, taught beside a field, at a wedding, on the road. Examples of his use of persons or situations or things as illustrations of his message are so numerous, one cannot fail to admit his absorption in the here and now and marvel at his skill in taking advantage of whatever was at hand in order to make a point. We who are so afraid to use secular things in worship would do well to remember how Jesus himself used whatever was around him to communicate the power and presence of his word: the fig tree, the field white for the harvest, the sower and his seed, the storm and the sea, the woman at the well, the woman caught in adultery, the woman caressing his feet with her tears and her hair, the little child, the beggar, a paralytic, a withered hand, his relatives, the herd of swine, the bushel, the lamp, salt, sheep, goats, a millstone, a woman's hemorrhage, loaves and fishes, a wedding feast, a coin, yeast, a mustard seed, a net, a pearl, blindness, deafness, leprosy, death. These and so many more things became part of the setting in which Jesus chose to teach, in fact became the means of his message.

To worship is to keep God's word, to seek a loving relationship with the Father through the Son. A solid relationship depends on a healthy self-image. "I am the bread of life" (John 6:35), said Jesus, "I am the light of the world" (8:12), "I am the gate" (10:9 JB), "I am the good shepherd" (10:11), "I am the resurrection" (11:25), "I am the way, and the truth, and the life" (14:6), "I am the true vine" (15:1), "before Abraham ever was, I Am" (8:58 JB), "Who do men say that I am? . . . Who do you say that I am?" (Mark 8:27-29)

At the heart of our inability to worship lies a crisis of identity. The Word helps me discover who God is and who I am: a child of God, heir to the promise, a little less than the angels, and a whole lot more than dust. Religion insists on separating what God died to join. Worship today struggles to put the world back together in the spirit of Jesus who sacralized the secular and disarmed the unsuspecting by identifying with their interests before hammering home his point. In some cases the punch line was so subtle that twenty centuries later, we have yet to get the message: that in Jesus the divine comes to terms with the human, tells us to love the flesh even as we transcend it, tells us to look at all that God has made and know that it is indeed "very good" (Gen. 1:31).

Remember me, Jesus said, as he broke bread with his friends. Soon after that, he died. In East Africa they will insist that a person is not really dead as long as someone who loves remembers. We do not depart from the earth until our last living, loving relation dies. All these centuries later, we who love the Lord gather to remember. He is there in the remembering, and his Spirit enables us to hand that memory on. No one inherits faith by hearsay. It has to be experienced, not as dogma, but event. This happens in liturgical worship which does so much more than link us to all who repeated its ritual, century upon past century. It recreates the dynamics of faith for this generation and the next.

Some years ago, when guitar-accompanied music was still new and people were still nervous, a small group of us took our song to a church one evening to demonstrate, outside of an actual service, the potential for prayer in this new musical style. At the conclusion of a rather spirited "Holy, holy, holy . . . blessed is he who comes in the name of the Lord," a voice shouted into the shocked silence: "If you really understood what was happening in the liturgy when you sing that song, you wouldn't get so excited!" "Sir," I replied, "we do understand what is happening in the liturgy, and that's why we get so excited!"

The addition of a human touch to worship does not mean reducing mystery to something we can completely comprehend. The sense of mystery deepens with ritual rightly done. "O wonderful exchange! The Creator of all, having assumed a living body, enriched us with divinity!" So sings the first antiphon at Lauds on the first day of January. Authentic worship is the precarious balance between ourselves and God, a touch of the human touched by the divine. We lift up lives of clay to transcendence that we might be fired into vessels worthy of receiving God. Continuity is crucial to lives defined by change. We cannot rid ourselves of ritual, or chaos will ensue. Instead we must authenticate rites of worship as a framework for free prayer.

Fixed forms contribute an essential psychological security to times of anxiety and flux. Their cyclical repetition cushions the shock of rapid change bombarding our every turn. Cult is sensible ritual when people express the content of their lives so that God can impress upon those same lives the content of belief. To keep clear of rigid formulas, we fill fixed forms with free expression, finding those spaces in worship appropriate for sharing our capacities to edify and inspire. This can happen more easily if we resume the liturgical attitude of the very early church, with less of an emphasis on role and a deeper appreciation of gift. Let our preaching return to its primary purpose—to inform, instruct, inspire. Sermons and homilies should present God's word to us as it was then and is now, utilizing the tools of biblical science to shape our understanding of historical context and give scope for present application. Slowly we must broaden participation in that ministry of the Word, confident that the Spirit still speaks through the mouths of babes and that young men and women who see visions and old people who dream dreams, and share them, can edify others and motivate many to live more serious lives. To look across the aisle of your church and hear someone you thought was indifferent suddenly share a piece of the Word as it touched one human life is to experience a new kind of power. A community, under the guidance of a skilled leader, can grope and grow together in an internalization of the good news. The insight of one will differ from that of another, and the richness of the Word, never fully expounded, will overwhelm with its potential to touch so many lives in so many different ways.

The role of the ministry here is to set the tone, the focus, the exegetical basis, then enable and sum up the sharing. Such preaching and prayer is a living testament to the relevance of the gospel now. It could lead to a definite change of heart. It might melt that stiff, icy gesture of the recently restored Greeting of Peace into a holy kiss, might enable us to circumvent our discomfort and the awkward restraint of a wooden pew to extend a warm and genuine welcome to the fellowship of Christ. We might even admit our need for reconciliation and change our mumbled "Lord, have mercy"—once, twice, three times—to a real cry for forgiveness, not for some vague and generalized sin, but for named and numbered failings. We might even turn from God to one another, to forgive and be forgiven. Then, like a clap of thunder, might "all the people say, 'Amen!'" (Ps. 106:48).

"Something which has existed since the beginning, that we have heard, that we have seen with our own eyes; that we have watched and touched with our hands: the Word, who is life—this is our subject" (I John 1:1 JB). Again and again we turn to the living Word, the bread of life. Here Protestants and Catholics can help each other by sharing the richness of their traditions and their different points of view. To Protestants the Word is central. This conviction can help Catholics develop a dynamic Liturgy of the Word based on solid exegesis properly proclaimed. The Catholic love for Eucharist can help Protestants rediscover meaningful communion through frequent breaking of bread.

The thrust of all our ritual is the building up of the community in the spirit of the early church. The means we use to edify and inspire must therefore be pastorally appropriate to any given group. What fits one community will not fit another. The process of prayer together must be constantly redesigned since the process is for us. "Always there remains this need to explain to each other that we are good. We all have a constant need to be reaffirmed. The single [person] needs this. The whole human race needs a yea, needs the large ceremonial pat on the back that says: Come on, come on! We can make it!"[6] Such worship is more than fellowship for all its communal emphasis. The goal of every gathering is to break open the hearts of those gathered, to lift up our spirits collectively to the One whose love draws us together in gratitude and praise. God is always the why of worship. It is the how that is meant for us.

3

YOU SHALL
HAVE A SONG

Speed. Stealth. Terror.
Pack quickly. Grab some of
that gold. Gather the children,
the herds, clothing. Don't wait
for the bread to rise! Hurry!
Run! It is the night long awaited,
the night of the great escape.
After four hundred years of
slavery, the children of Israel
are running for their lives.
There was need for haste. Pharaoh
may have given permission for the
departure, but he had changed his
mind before. He would fluctuate
again. There was barely time to
taste the freedom when Egyptian
troops tracked the fleeing refugees
down, cornering them encamped
against the water's edge. Once
again the fear. Once again the
terror. No way out this time but
the leap into the path of miracle.
Forward! It's shallow here,
passable there. Quickly, the Lord
is making a way through the water,

carving out a passage to the other
side. But look! Back there!
Stuck in the mud, tossed by the
sudden wind whipping the waters
into a fury, sinking, sinking. . . .
The pursuers have disappeared.
Captivity is over. Free at last!

Safe, dazed, delivered, the Israelites begin to sing:
"Sing to the Lord, for he has triumphed gloriously;
the horse and his rider he has thrown into the sea"
(Exod. 15:21). A few lines, lifting the heart high and
higher. Miriam's song. The community's song, sung
again and again and again. A song of the very
moment, rising out of the mud and the miracle of
newly liberated lives. Then Miriam, still leading the
song of the people, takes up her timbrel, and all the
women take up their timbrels, and they dance.
Have you ever wondered how and why the
women of Israel remembered to bring their tambourines? It had been a night of urgency and terror.
There was no time to make lists or to plan. All
attention was centered on the safety of the children,
bread for the journey, only those essentials that
could be carried on the run, yet the women opted to
take their tambourines. Not one or two women only,
not just the musically inclined, but enough women
to justify the phrase written long, long after: "and all
the women" followed Miriam with dancing and with
tambourines. How vital must music have been to the
life of that community when instruments were
considered something that one could not do without.
For that matter, have you ever stopped to consider

72

Miriam's song? Mud-spattered and still shaken, the people let out a shout of praise, not a hymn precisely metered, previously written and previously approved, but a song spilling forth word by rugged word, telling in human sounds and syllables of an event already sacred. Can you even imagine Miriam at that moment calling out to the crowd gathered there in prayer: "Turn to Number 99 in your hymnals, please, Hymn 99"? Can you picture those people restraining their enthusiasm until the entire melody had been stated on the accompanist's wooden flute? How does one normally respond to a narrow escape from death or four hundred more years of slavery? It must have been a loud, emotional, undisciplined, full of feeling kind of song. It must have been a song appropriate to a decisive experience of God.

Turbulent years later, the children of Israel had again crossed safely over, this time into the land of promise. Again God delivers them. We hear of another song. Sisera, commander of the Canaanite army, persecutor of the Jewish people, is suddenly on the defensive. In the heat of battle, he seeks asylum in the tent of the lady Jael. Safe for the moment and thoroughly exhausted, he falls soundly asleep. Jael slays him with a tent peg driven smartly through his skull. The news spreads quickly. "Awake, awake, Deborah! Awake, awake, strike up a song" (Judg. 5:12). Deborah, prophetess and judge in the land of Israel, comes before the people assembling to give thanks for yet another victory of the Lord. They sang a song that day, we are told. Listen to some of the words from an ancient liturgical celebration of that event.

73

She struck Sisera, crushed his head,
pierced his temple and shattered it.
At her feet he tumbled, he fell, he lay;
at her feet he tumbled, he fell.
Where he tumbled, there he fell dead.

(Judg. 5:26-27 JB)

A violent song, not exactly the kind that could slip unchallenged into the hymnals of today. Because the text and its tone are so foreign to our own religious response, our first reaction is to dismiss the passage and insist that this piece of Scripture simply does not apply. Yet the song has been handed down to us within the context of God's word, so it must have some meaning. Arising out of a different culture at a distant point in time, the message could well be that relevant prayer-songs cannot continue from one generation to the next, from one culture to another, cannot pass without alteration into a stranger's corporate praise. Rather like the so-called Song of Deborah, cult songs reflect a particular culture at a particular time.

Raise a song, sound the timbrel,
the sweet lyre with the harp.
Blow the trumpet at the new moon.

(Ps. 81:2-3)

Song was a part of Jewish prayer because song was a part of Jewish life. There were work songs and harvest songs; songs for weddings, banquets, and funerals; victory songs similar to the two we have already seen. Jubilant, the people greeted David's triumph over Goliath with tambourine and lyre and dancing. "Saul has killed his thousands, and David his ten thousands" (I Sam. 18:7), they sang, over and over again. Jubilant, David and all the house of Israel accompanied the ark of God, "making merry before the Lord . . . with songs and lyres and harps and tambourine and castenets and cymbals" (II Sam. 6:5). But before he could celebrate that hour, David must lament the deaths of Saul and Jonathan. "How did the heroes fall?" (1:19 JB), he mourned, punctuating his dirge with that plaintive, heartbroken refrain. Small snatches of life, from Isaiah's Song of the Vineyard (chap. 5) to the wedding music of the Song of Songs, snatches of life intensely experienced, these are the mode of the people's prayer. The Psalms substantiate this. "I will sing to the Lord as long as I live; I will sing praise to my God while I have being" (Ps. 104:33). Songs of praise, lament, thanks-giving, trust, songs of individuals and of groups gathered together to pray, the Psalms demonstrate with conviction how closely knit were the prayer-songs of the people to life, to the land, to the Lord. Songs springing from raw reality, from the pain of exile, the joy of deliverance, the fear of death, these formed the basis of Israelite cultic response. In fact, these would inadvertently become the prime cult songs of the future, claimed by Christians convinced that their rote repetition was undoubtedly a more perfect prayer than anything the modern mind might imagine.

What a long and difficult journey from the banks of the Red Sea to the threshold of the twentieth-century congregational church. On the perilous march through history, God continued to intervene in the lives of people, but circumstances invariably arose to alter their corresponding songs. The vitality of those

75

early shouts of praise finds little echo in much of the church's music today. Where was the critical juncture, what was the decisive influence that so determined the shape of the Christian's cultic song?

During the time between the two Testaments, definite musical patterns prevailed. Set structures form the framework for the canticles chronicled in Luke. Free and full of feeling, the texts are still an authentic, immediate response to God's intervening deed. "My heart is overflowing with praise of my Lord, my soul is full of joy in God my Saviour" (Luke 1:46-47 Phillips). The cry of Zechariah follows close on Mary's song, hymning the marvels awaiting the child that he too is promised. "And you, little child, will be called the prophet of the Most High; for you will go before the Lord to prepare the way for his coming." (v. 76 Phillips) Then we hear the song of Simeon, praising the God who has allowed him to witness this moment of grace. "Now, Lord, you are dismissing your servant in peace, as you promised! For with my own eyes I have seen your salvation which you have made ready for all peoples to see—a light to show truth to the gentiles and bring glory to your people Israel" (2:29-32 Phillips). These songs of surprise, Spirit-inspired grace set structures with new modes of meaning.

This tradition of song continues as a New Testament expression of faith. Scriptural exegetes have verified the existence of many early Christian hymns, like the Logos hymn that forms the prelude to the Gospel according to John. It sings of the light that enhanced our darkness, the Word now flesh who endured indifference to bear witness to truth and grace. This verse heralds a similar theme: "He was made visible in the flesh, attested by the Spirit, seen by the angels, proclaimed to the pagans, believed in by the world, taken up in glory" (I Tim. 3:16 JB). The Second Letter to Timothy preserves this passage: "If we have died with him, then we shall live with him. If we hold firm, then we shall reign with him. If we disown him, then he will disown us. We may be unfaithful, but he is always faithful" (II Tim. 2:11-13 JB). Imagine how this hymn must have resounded through the assembly, communicating that enthusiasm immune to every effort to contain its spread. Melodies, meters, even the specific meaning of the words have been lost to us, but these and other textual fragments are enough to indicate that singing was indeed a dynamic dimension of the primitive church, the sign of a loving fellowship alienated from society and bonded closely together in a common experience of the risen Lord. "Be filled with the Spirit, addressing one another in psalms and hymns and inspired songs. Sing praise to the Lord with all your hearts" (Eph. 5:18-19). Psalms, hymns, inspired songs. What meaning lies secretly hidden in this mysterious phrase? The Psalms we know from the Bible. We have hints of New Testament hymns. But what about the songs? Was this simply a poetic expression, or was there really a delineation of musical forms in the early church? Perhaps more than in any other area, contemporary church music might best be served by some insight into the style and content of those inspired songs.

"Late that night Paul and Silas were praying and singing God's praises, while the other prisoners listened" (Acts 16:25 JB). By the time Paul and Silas were imprisoned together in Macedonia, there was probably a whole repertoire of songs and hymns uniquely Christian, for those lyrical snatches that Scripture contains date from a period prior to the formulation of the Gospels or even the writings of Paul. So accustomed was the early church to song and to singing that Ignatius, Bishop of Antioch, could address the community at Ephesus in musical metaphor at the century's close, confident that through this image they would not miss his very pertinent point.

Your presbytery, indeed, which deserves its name and is a credit to God, is closely tied to the bishop as the strings to a harp. Wherefore your accord and harmonious love is a hymn to Jesus Christ. Yes, one and all, you should form yourselves into a choir, so that, in perfect harmony and taking your pitch from God, you may sing in unison and with one voice to the Father through Jesus Christ.

Further evidence of an established tradition of cultic song surfaces not long after in a letter of the official Pliny to the Emperor Trajan (*ca.* A.D. 112) describing some of the practices of the suspicious sect. "They asserted, however, that the amount of their fault or error was this: that they had been accustomed to assemble on a fixed day before daylight and sing by turns [i.e., antiphonally] a hymn to Christ as God." The impact of shared song can be imagined, a source of strength and inspiration during periods of persecution, fostering an élan within a community that grew in numbers every day. But song during that first century had an added purpose, more pragmatic in its intent. An effective force for shaping attitudes, song was one way of instructing the membership in the fundamentals of belief. Christological conceptions gradually reveal the nature of Jesus' messianic mission, the suffering and glorified servant of Yahweh who, in the symbolic lyric of the book of Revelation, becomes the Paschal lamb slain for the redemption of the world and now enthroned at the right hand of God. Many of those early hymn fragments reflect this desire to inform or to refute, boldly attempting to weave the threads of evolving doctrine into a pattern demanding assent.

> His state was divine,
> yet he did not cling
> to his equality with God
> but emptied himself
> to assume the condition of a slave,
> and became as men are;
> and being as all men are,
> he was humbler yet,
> even to accepting death,
> death on a cross. (Phil. 2:6-8 JB)

How stark the contrast between this text and the tone of Miriam's song! The style continues in the so-called Colossian hymn.

> He is the image of the unseen God
> and the first-born of all creation,
> for in him were created
> all things in heaven and on earth:
> everything visible and everything invisible,
> Thrones, Dominations, Sovereignties, Powers.
> (Col. 1:15, 16 JB)

What is characteristic here? Certainly not a sharing of daily ups and downs, no prayer of the present moment addressed to a familiar God. We encounter instead two hymns that are extremely dogmatic, promulgating a theology that had better be believed. There is a shift in emphasis from songs that arise out of life lived to those that will shape life accordingly. Strongly doctrinal hymns engage the head more than the heart. Christianity has always been much too serious, suspicious of the dancing, skeptical of celebrations expressed in human terms. Yet the Christ of Christianity is God-made-flesh, validating all that is human. Why then did so many early hymns hail him as Lamb enthroned, worthy of our homage, mysterious and remote? Isn't it ironic that we who know a man-God prefer a "sacred" song? By ignoring the touchingly human Lord of history, we in fact missed the point. Yet all through the struggling centuries, the sound of that different drummer teased with a different beat.

For the first two centuries, intense persecution plagued the infant church. The annals of the martyrs show that time and time again, Christians went into the arena singing, and only death could silence their song. They sang with a simple solid faith, unshaken in the hope that the Lord eagerly awaited the one who victoriously endured. The Edict of Milan (A.D. 313) changed everything with its promise of peace at last. Christianity was finally legal. The persecuted could come up out of the catacombs into the full light of day. No more hiding. No more fighting to survive. But as often happens in an institution, the energy that went toward survival now focused on finding a system for continuing what had been salvaged at so great a cost. It was time for structuring ways of best preserving and perpetuating the faith. The legiti-mate church banned instrumental music from its ritual, for surely its pagan overtones made it unfit for the public praise of God. The Council of Laodicea (A.D. 364) went a step further, reserving for the clergy the right to sing during the official liturgy—a special group for singing within a special liturgical rite and soon a special kind of music, the natural outcome of an attitude that looked upon worship as something set apart. From the fourth century forward, the seeds of the sacred-versus-secular struggle sink deep, persistent roots, creating a dichotomy that remained unshaken until the last two dozen years.

History credits Ambrose, late fourth-century Bishop of Milan, with the first of the church modes that form the basis of plainsong in the West. Ambrose also contributed the poetic, metrical hymn to the treasury of the Western church and reintroduced the custom of antiphonal or responsive singing. The writings of Ambrose, Augustine, and John Chrysostom contain much information on the musical attitudes and practices of their day. For now it is enough to know that modal music flourished in the Middle Ages, yielding many different chants within the many Christian communities that spread far and wide. Within the limits of the modes there was freedom, freedom to express the text in one's own language and in one's own style. But this phase of relative freedom was to end with Gregory, the early seventh-century reformer, later heralded as Gregory the Great. Gregory's system of standardization affected all singing in all communities of the universal church. There was no developed notation at that time, consequently, music was not yet written down, yet Gregory spearheaded a review of the many chants that were popularly in use. He

81

evaluated, sifted, selected, then promulgated one system of chant, the Roman chant, chanted in the Latin language, for universal use. What followed for several hundred years was the golden age of chant. It was a tarnished age for the worshiper. Music in liturgies outside of Rome now called for a language people did not understand. Individuality slipped one notch nearer death with this impersonal, legalistic blow. Where conformity prevailed, the worship experience moved one step further in fact and in feeling from its participating people. A process of selection insures that only the best survives. We inherited a superior music under the label of Gregorian chant, a music that celebrates an ideal wedding of melody and word, a music whose genius and sheer beauty has seldom been surpassed. But selection stifles the spirit, especially when it silences what it considers to be the forbidden song.

Law crushes creativity, but seldom for very long. Church restrictions led to the evolution of a new musical style in the world outside the sanctuary. The single, unharmonized line gave way to a polyphonic form. The dream of several simultaneous voices weaving intricate patterns of sound enticed the church musician to explore this delicious, secular source. As is true of most beginnings, the style in transition was somewhat austere. But the open interval tonality of organum quickly passed into richer, warmer harmonies as the secular ars nova washed over the Western world, sweeping even the church's staunch sense of separation along in its wake. Secular influences chipped away at sacred music, a characteristic that the church, despite its many determined efforts, could never really shake.

Already in the fourteenth century, music reflected the revolt against Latin that had been slowly gaining ground. Succeeding centuries spawned a choral music that tried to bridge the breach between liturgy and life. Loyal church composers often borrowed current popular tunes from secular sources around which they would weave the musical devices of their day. By the fifteenth century, this sacred song with several voice parts, the polyphonic motet, showed great rhythmic freedom. There was definite syncopation and a hint of the chordal progression that underlies modern music. Choirs flourished, skillfully presenting a choral church music that offered so wide a choice. The path of the evolving motet was not an easy one. There were abuses. Results were often poor, even disastrous. Borrowed texts, tunes, themes invoked a questionable response. Garbled texts, resulting from the mesh of several languages all sung at the same time, rendered the ritual word of God incomprehensible. There were moments of absolute madness, but there were moments too of sheer genius. Textbooks on music history pay tribute to those who briefly but brilliantly graced the choral scene with meaning. One of these was Palestrina, whose sixteenth-century Renaissance motets signify a watershed, a climax, of choral music in the Catholic church. Various artistic streams had trickled through those post-Gregorian centuries. Yet for all the attempts at alteration, the church's ritual music remained amazingly intact. Until those final hours before the dawn of the Reformation, its song was sung in a borrowed tongue. Foreign phrases emphasized a sense of the majestic and the sacred. Musical renditions were the property of a particular group of people set apart and quite aloof from the maddened crowd.

The consequence of all this? Inevitable, it would seem. "You shall have a song as in the night when a holy feast is kept; and gladness of heart, as when one sets out to the sound of the flute to go to the mountain of the Lord" (Isa. 30:29). Silenced in the church, the people elected to sing outside. Folk music, the song of the people, flourished. Historians list over fourteen hundred religious songs in the German language that arose during those centuries preceding the Reformation. Sacred hymns. Secular religious songs. Carols, or sacred folk songs, that emerged from the liturgical dramas and mystery plays of the day. Mary songs, inspired by an age of chivalry that extolled the qualities of woman. In contrast to contemporary experience, songwriting at that time followed different rules. Surprisingly, one did not have to write a whole new tune. Writing a song meant rewriting the words to a song already written, maybe changing a note or two, maybe not. Street songs, love songs, even drinking songs supplied the melodic framework supporting religious texts. These songs had much influence, for they were sung everywhere: on pilgrimage, at work, at recreation, in the classroom, sometimes even at the end of the service in church. They were sung for the sincere joy of singing. Some texts sheltered errant doctrine. To offset their influence, occasionally the clergy took up the pen and wrote some corrective songs of their own.

There is no discrediting the impact of the vernacular—the popular language—on the psyche of a people. John Huss, precursor of the Reformation, understood this. His congregations in Bohemia had a large vernacular hymnody, sung not by a choir, but by all the people. These hymns were bound into books before his death in 1415. Due recognition must be given to the congregational hymns of Huss and to that rich heritage of secular religious song if we would understand the stark transition from one form of sacred music to another in the vanguard of protest and reform. For the new music of the Reformation represents no sudden break with the past, but rather a gradual takeover of a style that had already become firmly fixed in the hearts of a religious people. It is in this context that we praise Luther's musical contribution to the future.

Martin Luther will always be remembered for his courageous stance against a thousand years of clerical control over the liturgy's ritual song, a stance that brought to an abrupt end, a thousand years of ritual silence on the part of a song-loving people. We call him the father of evangelical hymnody, a title he richly deserves. He did not give birth to the vernacular congregational hymn. We have seen how it developed before him. He validated it, enabled it to come into its own, to come in from the fields and the forests, to cross the threshold of the house of God. He encouraged his congregations to respond to the Word heard at long last in familiar, everyday accents, to respond with an outpouring of praise. It was indeed a new song, a song whose tone resembles with aching similarity Catholic liturgical reform some four hundred years after Luther's passing.

The gospel was central to Luther's sense of song and a felt need for adequate materials drove him to try his own hand at writing. A gifted musician himself, he wrote a total of thirty-six hymns. Of these, scholarship credits him with three original hymn tunes. The others he adapted or rearranged for use according to the practice prevalent at that time. His writings reflected the influence of his love for the liturgical cycle and the ritual of the old church. His hymns echoed the sound of current Catholic music, but their texts held different meanings. Luther's contribution to the whole domain of church music was immense. He supported congregational singing without demeaning the role of the choir. He took an innovative stand, upholding the right of musicians to an adequate income guaranteed by the church. The hymns he wrote or authorized contributed greatly to the swift spread of Reformation doctrine, assuring the illiterate masses, who learned song after song by rote, of at least a tentative grasp on shifting formulas of belief. Song became a powerful tool once again for edging whole hordes of people toward a particular conviction. The songs of the Reformation rallied the people, reflected their protest against age-old norms, and initiated an irrevocable surge toward wholeness in the worshiping community.

The audacity of Martin Luther resulted in some turbulent years in the history of the Christian church. Having once stormed the apparently impregnable deposit of faith, the onslaught continued with terrifying ferocity as a barrage of protest welled up, spilled over, and spread. In a way, church music bore the brunt of the new experimental mood. In Switzerland there was a reaction to Luther's German Reformation which continued to cherish so much of the past, retaining chants, some Latin, even ritual feasts and patterns. The new movement was characterized from the outset by an austerity of style and practice. It tried to ban all music in one swift, violent stroke. In 1524, the influential Ulrich Zwingli took a stand against the playing of organs in the city of Zurich. As a result, organs were smashed and all choral music discontinued. Ironically, Zwingli was an accomplished musician, a composer, and a skilled performer on most instruments of his day. Yet a distrust of the human dimension, a distrust that has cursed Christianity throughout its history, drove him to eliminate the precious gift of music from the service of the church.

There was more sense and sensitivity in John Calvin who followed after. He too was skeptical of secular trappings, especially of those popular hymns of human contrivance, yet he understood that the prayer of a people is stifled with the stilling of their song. Zwingli's solution was certainly not working. Antiphonal recitation was too sophisticated for a congregation that lacked an educational background. Already the clergy had taken over the people's part, a rather bizarre twist for a group formed in protest to that very practice. Something had to be done.

Calvin's solution was the metrical psalm. Opposed to instrumental music and to choral singing, intolerant of the popular hymn that dared substitute the words of creatures for the word of God, Calvin was convinced that the canonical psalms were the acceptable, in fact the only, mode of praise. His small book of metrical psalms, published in 1539, inaugurated a new style of sacred singing. These first seventeen psalms, five of which were probably

Calvin's own musical compositions, made universal congregational participation possible and quickly became characteristic of Reformed worship. Simple metrical melodies featured one musical note for every syllable of text. A classic example has been preserved in the tune known as Old Hundreth, familiar to many as the popular doxology, "Praise God from Whom All Blessings Flow." Sung unaccompanied, in unison, in the language of the people, the sixteenth-century metrical psalm had the whole scope of the psalter for variety, yet its metered rhythm established a pattern that was fairly easy to master. Weekly hymn sings, to which we trace the hymn board, a fixture in contemporary churches, enabled the metrical style of singing to take hold and to continue unchallenged for nearly 150 years. Most people would agree that a special gift of Protestants is a familiarity with the psalms. For this, all traditions owe a lot to the musical commitment of John Calvin.

In 1520, the Anabaptists stepped gingerly into the ecclesiastical arena. By 1535, they were all but annihilated. Why? Except for some short-lived splinter groups with lunatic tendencies, they were a peace-loving people, politically passive, dedicated to the pursuit of principle without force. Coming out of the Zwingli movement, their life-style and worship sought to recapture the spirit of the early apostolic church, naming the New Testament as their sole source of faith and practice. Love was the measure of their actions. Love was the distinguishing theme of their songs. Yet they were persecuted relentlessly by the other churches, treated as scum or refuse, always, of course, in the name of the Lord. Imprisonment. Banishment. Death. The Anabaptists bore it all in the spirit of that younger church they so desired to emulate. Similar to those earlier martyrdoms, bitter persecution yielded a sweeter song.

As some of them lay in grievous imprisonment, they sang hymns of praise to God, as those who are in great joy. Some did likewise as they were being led out to death and the place of persecution; as those going to meet the bridegroom at a wedding, they sang out joyfully with uplifted voice.[1]

The short, intense Anabaptist presence sparked an explosion of song.

A flood of religious songs poured over the young brotherhood like a vivifying and refreshing stream. The songs became the strongest attractive force for the brotherhood. They sang themselves into the hearts of many, clothed in popular tunes. They were mostly martyr songs, which breathed an atmosphere of readiness to die and a touching depth of faith.[2]

Records list 130 Anabaptist hymn writers by name and over a thousand Anabaptist hymns. Long, crude, repetitious, some songs were ballads, others chronicled news or those historic events worth recording, still others spilled forth defiantly as a living witness to a faith worth dying for. The sincere outpourings of the heart that mark Anabaptist hymnody substantiate the view that hymnbooks are an accurate index of theological formulation, or the lack of it, and that folk song is the articulation of the people. The Amish, who continue the Anabaptist tradition along with the Mennonites, still use the four-hundred-year-old Anabaptist hymnbook, the *Ausbund.* It is the oldest post-Reformation hymnal in continuous use down through the present day. We might glean this insight from the Anabaptists and their struggle, in order that their passing might not have been in vain. It is best expressed in the words of Paul Miller, who writes:

Anabaptists insisted that a follower of Christ lives in the Spirit and walks in the Spirit constantly, and that worship is not an isolated hour when one strains to realize the fullness and nearness of the life of God. For them life was a preparation for worship more than worship a preparation for life.[3]

A quick glance at religious music from the Reformation to the twentieth century reveals a tangle of growth and development. Fertile imaginations fashioned forms that became more and more complex, more and more emotionally appealing. These burgeoned and spread, choking any lingering association with liturgical discretion. The Catholic church clung to its Latin chants and motets sung by specially trained choirs, although by the end of the seventeenth century, the proximity of an alternative had its effect as German hymns slipped into use at the so-called Song Mass. On the other side of the ecclesiastical chasm, congregational hymns, metrical psalms, and simply religious songs, all in the language of the people, led to the full flowering of a distinctly Protestant music. In the Lutheran tradition, a choir began to assist the congregation by adding harmony to the tune. The organ augmented and eventually displaced the choir through the sheer persistence of its own harmonic strength. Solo singing took precedence over choral works, the new major-minor tonality replaced the distinctive modality of chant, and accompaniments became more elaborate until instrumental music emerged as an art form all its own. Church music became extremely flamboyant, often losing sight of the purpose of its reform, until that eighteenth-century giant, Johann Sebastian Bach, blessed the world with his creative genius. His chorales, cantatas, preludes, and fugues exude a religious quality as yet unsurpassed.

In England, Isaac Watts published *Hymns and Spiritual Songs* in 1707. It proved to be a turning point, earning him acclaim as founder of English hymnody. Mid-century influence belongs to the brothers Wesley, John and Charles. Charles was an especially prolific and gifted hymn writer in the revival meeting tradition of singing, responsible for something like 6,500 hymns. Many of his texts are still among the best-loved expressions of contemporary Methodist faith. Anglican chant also reached a high degree of excellence and served its congregations well. The anthem of the Anglican liturgy, a short choral piece similar to both the German cantata and the medieval Latin motet, is still an alternative to the congregational hymn.

In America, the seventeenth-century Puritan psalmody, dependent on an oral tradition, gradually disappeared. The Great Awakening, an eighteenth-century mass movement inspired by the fiery oratory of itinerant preachers, launched a rash of new sects from already dissenting groups. Moravians, who were descendants of the Bohemian Brethren of John Huss, and Shakers were especially noted for their highly distinctive musical styles. Out West, particularly in California, Spanish missionaries kept Catholic church music from liturgical disintegration.

Elsewhere, however, an overwhelming Protestant presence was bound to affect the neighbors with its abundance of appealing songs. Bereft of a musical culture, isolated Catholic parishes soon identified with the sound of the day, ornamenting their liturgy with what often amounted to artistic or purely emotional displays. For Protestants, the nineteenth-century sound was the gospel song, a religious counterpart to the sentimental secular ballad. Subjective, highly imaginative, these songs became the backbone of evangelistic efforts and were a success as teaching aids. It did not seem to matter that the tunes were often cheap, the language excessive, the theology bad or inaccurate. Gospel songs fanned the fire of emotion at a time when emotion scored high. Crowds of people responded to their direct appeal at the rallies of Dwight L. Moody and Ira D. Sankey. Songs poured from the pen of Sankey to stir souls to fervor and to elicit a rededication of the heart. Where the gospel song served as the service song, church music remained destitute of liturgical propriety. A whole era seemed to have forgotten the essentials of Protestant reform. With the Civil War composers, who wrote both war songs and church songs, militant images crossed over into religious songs. Strong religious vibrations accompanied the nadir of liturgical song, a warning that spiritual goodwill and artistry do not necessarily go hand in hand.

After the Civil War, the North discovered the song of the South, caught a glimpse of the black's ability to bind together environment, experience, and a religious intuition with integrity in stirring songs of praise. Rising out of the pathos of the human condition, the spirituals delight in hints of heavenly glory, imaginative escapes to the Promised Land, unwavering faith in the mercies of Jesus, and in all the promises of Christ. Within the Catholic context, there was already in that century the feel of new beginnings, the rumblings of reform. Earlier, the Caecilian movement began to exert an influence in German-speaking countries with its efforts to revive classical polyphony and restore an interest in liturgical chant. Reform was clearly necessary, even though ritually speaking, nothing much had changed. Through the years, the chant's meaning within the liturgical framework had been lost. No doubt, for liturgy had maintained its distance from the worshiper, fostering ritual confusion as the priest repeated verbally those parts of the Mass that the choir had already sung, in time negating the choir's role. Chant selections were far too often truncated versions that had survived centuries of revision. Then, of course, there was that irresistable vernacular song so prominent in Protestant and secular circles. The desire to develop new a cappella pieces, new instrumentally accompanied works and vernacular hymns suitable for extraliturgical services caused the movement to spread rapidly throughout Europe and into America. Gaining official church sanction, it set about its task with determination. The results, however, failed to measure up. Scores of composers submitted works, and the flurry of publication produced a landslide of poor music that overshadowed works of real value. Instead of liturgical depth, superficiality hindered the movement's very aim. A push for objectivity led to rigidity. The grass-roots movement evolved into an officially approved institution bent on perpetuating ecclesiastical values, and died.

Others were also caught up in the climate of reform. Research into the history of hymnody resulted in a revival of many old yet significant hymns. The Benedictine monks of Solesme in France labored to restore the chant to its original vitality, tracing individual pieces through multiple editings to their source. The publication of their scholarly research eventually formed the basis for the Vatican edition of the chant in this century, available to chant enthusiasts as the *Liber Usualis,* one more phase in its promulgation before it finally faded from prominence before the force of twentieth-century demands. There were many simultaneous attempts to revitalize the chant, too numerous to mention here. General disagreement in approach and system caused this common thrust to work at cross-purposes, so that the versions available for practical use never achieved that widespread acceptance all reformers so deeply desired. This conglomerate of attempts and trends, then, this mixture of true quality with devotional trivia, swirled about the liturgical doorposts as Pope Pius X issued his *Motu Proprio* on sacred music on November 22, 1903, ushering in an era of such sweeping change that no stretch of the imagination could ever have foreseen. That predictable giant, the Catholic Church, inert for so many centuries, was aroused at long last. Once fully awakened, it would rattle and shake those carefully arranged structures until the walls came tumbling down.

All change begins well in advance of its general implementation. Vatican II brought to fruition efforts that began more than a century before, fulfilling expectations with a certain surprising twist. The clamor for an authentic people's song was given new impetus as the century rounded the corner and entered the people's age. In a way, Pius X was ahead of his time. Inherent in his outmoded recommendations was the spark that could ignite the imaginations of the world. This was far from obvious. In fact, to the modern mind, he seems to have missed the point. Using traditional terminology and structure, he warned anew that sacred music must be holy, a reminder that rings hollow when linked to a rite from which all touches of the human had long since disappeared. But he cared, deeply cared, that his reign might see the rising of the congregation's song. He sincerely believed that the chant could be the vehicle of such a renaissance. "Special efforts are to be made to restore the use of the Gregorian chant by the people." The reason? "So that the faithful may again take a more active part." He did admit that it had been a long, long time since the chant had been the popular mode of praise, a practice stretching back into "ancient times" before "ecclesiastical offices" were erected to intone its pristine phrases. Throughout his instruction, Pius X opened doors a crack, sometimes flung them wide, then quickly nailed them shut again. He announced that "every nation is permitted to admit into its ecclesiastical compositions those special forms which may be said to constitute its native music," a radical permission at the time. But he added, "Still these forms must be subordinated in such a manner to the general characteristics of sacred music that nobody of any nation may receive an impression other than good on hearing

them." Bang. It is clear from historical precedent that
Rome writes the rules characterizing sacred music.
Enough said. It is very unclear how any nation's
indigenous music could communicate only good to
all people all over the world unless every listener
understood and appreciated that culture's mores and
the materials of its art. We are also reminded that

the Church has always recognized and favored the
progress of the arts [a point that could be vehemently
challenged], admitting to the service of religion everything good and beautiful discovered by genius in the
course of the ages [what wonderful news!]—always,
however, with due regard [and here it comes again] to the
liturgical laws.

The brackets of course are mine. Then a note of hope
for tomorrow: "Modern music is also admitted to the
Church, since it too furnishes compositions of such
excellence . . . that they are in no way unworthy of
the liturgical functions," that is, as long as they are
"not fashioned even in their external forms after the
manner of profane pieces." A good example of
ecclesiastical double-talk. The raw materials of
rhythm and tonality are fundamental to both sacred
and secular song. Further definitions emerge from a
discreet application of text, treatment, taste. Pius X's
preoccupation with preserving the laws of the
institutional church reflects that sacred/secular dichotomy that still haunts renewal attempts. His
personal tug-of-war is typical of the church's struggle
in this century: a daring step forward and a cautious
pulling back, an unleashing of the spirit that is
quickly harnessed by an already existing law. The
institutional church promulgated all the cautionary

points in the *Motu Proprio* of Pius X. The spirit church discerned the dynamism behind his thinking before his dreams were tempered by prudence and restraint or edited by an invisible curial hand. Today's music is trying to capture the intent of the real Pius X. Surely he would have rejoiced to see this day, gently blessing contemporary efforts to "pray in beauty" with a suitable liturgical song.

There was a genuine though half-hearted attempt to implement the recommendations of Pius X. It never got off the ground. Here and there, parishes actually tried to sing, but the chant was simply beyond them. It did not mean anything; it was lip homage without heart. Try to give life to a dead language, to get excited about what you do not understand. Some groups managed and even today are enthused. But by and large, it was left to the cathedral choir, the monastery, and the occasional convent chapel to recapture its spirit. There chant flourished and grew more lovely with every passing day. Meanwhile the people listened and waited and watched. It was the liturgists who finally concluded that there would be no genuine participation, so desired by Pius X, unless comprehension went hand in hand. People sing out of their own experience, use the only words they know when they cry out to their God. God understands all languages, people very few. Prayer is people in relation to God. Both need to understand. And so the time had come. Insights of early reformers finally penetrated Gothic walls.

It was a quiet surge forward, beginning in church basements, continuing behind closed doors. Small enclaves of scholars grew into larger groups of concerned persons gathered here and there. Texts of the liturgy were translated and tried, giving birth to that phenomenon known as the underground Mass. Vernacular phrases were set to music reminiscent of the chant. Steadily, convincingly, the liturgical movement grew and grew, fostered in this country by Dom Virgil Michel of St. John's Abbey, College-ville, Minnesota, nurtured by Godfrey Diekmann, O.S.B. and others too numerous to name, some of whom centered at Notre Dame's School of Liturgy in Indiana. After World War II, the movement took off. Planned liturgical weeks met annually around the country, increasing a hundredfold in attendance until thousands gathered together to learn about and to experience their projected future role in a liturgy they could understand, one that valued their presence, needed their voice. In 1955, the Theological College of Washington, D.C., prepared *The People's Hymnal* for use when and where permitted. The compilation of some of the best liturgical hymns from ancient, Reformation, and contemporary sources deleted once and for all, on principle, those saccharine, mediocre hymns that continued to stimulate Catholic devotion even after the White List of liturgically acceptable music was published by the Society of St. Gregory in 1928. A strong intuition of future needs inspired some excellent transition music, notably the psalm settings of Joseph Gelin-eau, the Jesuit liturgist and composer in France. Worldwide clamor for change gained momentum through unauthorized experimentation outside the structure of the parish Mass. Although the sweeping liturgical changes of the Second Vatican Council caught many by surprise, the Constitution on the Liturgy was simply an official amen to what was already a reality. It was the culmination of a determined, systematic return to the sources by restoring to the people their God-given right.

It is a God-given right to sing, to lift up our voices freely, to praise the "Thou" and affirm the "we" in a keen collective sound. Let us sing then with rejoicing. Let us praise with a mighty chorus the substance of our song. Liturgists greeted the new year with the enthusiasm of children. Their troubles were finally over. Anything was possible. It was 1965. Those who cared intensely about liturgy were the next in line to be shaken by surprise. It soon became apparent in those still silent churches that something was very wrong. People were allowed to participate, in fact, were strongly encouraged to participate in a new ritual they could now comprehend. Why, then, didn't they sing? It never occurred that after fifteen hundred years of conditioned silence, one could not simply legislate response. People were hurt and angry and dreadfully unprepared. First they were told to be silent. Now they were told to sing. Sing! Why? For what reason? They felt more like crying! Besides, they didn't know any songs. It was not an easy transition. In fact, looking back, one wonders how it could have been any worse. There was too little preparation, too little time for questions, no time at all for adjustment, just a long list of answers and one more set of rules. Gamely, people struggled to adapt to all that was new and different, stared at their celebrant now facing them, even tried to sing. Obviously, troubles were far from over. They had only just begun.

The second phase of the Catholic liturgical movement dates to that apparent loss of an entire musical heritage overnight. At the stroke of a clock, Latin chant, Latin hymns, classical polyphony, contemporary for centuries, seemed suddenly obsolete. One was no longer allowed even to "weep for mirth" with those sweet religious songs. Artistically impoverished, musically bankrupt, having inherited a goal with no objectives, where was the parish to turn? Feelings were still too raw to reach out to the rich repertoire of Reformation hymns. After all, common folk were visibly smarting under ritual changes that seemed Protestant enough! There was that experimental music, to be sure, but most of it was tired. Groups anticipating the changes had been singing those songs for years. Mass music was stiff and predictable, while deep down in the celebrative subconscious there teased that tantalizing beat and a childhood love for dancing. Rip Van Winkle had awakened, but oh, how the times had changed! Steel strings and skins captured radios that captivated minds. A folk-style music was sweeping the country. It was Peter, Paul, and Mary. It was ballad, bluegrass, rock. When the future writes our history, it is bound to note the mighty influence of the hootenanny on contemporary church song. The folk phenomenon was more than music. It was a whole new notion of community that gathered to sing, hour after hour, spirited, poignant songs. It was gently, sincerely descriptive and, with disarming honesty, gave birth to the modern song. Its singers were unafraid to question, comfortable with their feelings, with letting it all hang out. Cutting across the denominational spectrum, they were quick to make the comparison: why do we have such contagious music while our church has such deadly songs?

Shouldn't we be as enthusiastic Sunday morning as we are on Saturday night? Why do the media hold the copyrights to all the better tunes? What is wrong with rhythm? What is wrong with just being ourselves? There was only one conclusion. To participate meaningfully in worship, I need my kind of song. So here and there, nonprofessional persons, searching, sensitive persons, sang out into the vacuum a different kind of song. They were seldom the church musicians. They were the little people. They were the singers of songs. There was no conscious movement at first to communicate further change, just a desperate cry for wholeness, a craving to really pray. Every age has produced its songs and hymns when it felt the need to do so. There will always be new music. Why are we still surprised? It was a natural move from *Tantum Ergo* to "Joy Is Like the Rain."

How elusive is sacred song. Its history spans the ages, reaching back to primitive societies where musical sounds were deemed the proper language for communication with the gods. Ancient deity hymns foreshadow much of what has been summarized all too simply here, influencing the song of the First Testament people, which in turn shaped the song of the Christian church. It is enlightening to trace the thread of music through salvation history, scrutinizing its relationship to public prayer and its power to unravel the complex attitudes of the human heart. Yet sweeping surveys are foolhardy gestures. History cannot be contained. For every single statement there are one hundred contrary statements waiting in the wings; for every trend, a countertrend; for every example, a thousand others prepared to

101

discredit, substantiate, or condition some norm. The historical sketch I have presented in these pages resembles how it was. Certainly not all that there was, for often much was happening in those spaces between the lines. Still there is enough here to give some indication of behavior and response, to help us interpret the new song, no longer "sacred," of the contemporary church. Why history? Why do we need to know? Because we must keep in touch with our roots. If we would understand strange, new directions, we must look to our traditions, we must understand and honor the past. For the past is never over. It surfaces again and again, recycling each generation's dreams from remnants of the old. We will have a much better idea of where we are going if we have some idea where we have been, if we come to terms with the meaning behind decisive turning points, with the process behind decisions, with the feeling behind the facts. Long before Pope John XXIII or Pius X or even Martin Luther, the liturgical movement was already in vogue, preparing the Catholic community for what inevitably lay ahead. We cannot blame the sixties for slaying our favorite songs. After centuries of bitter separations, Catholics publicly thank Protestant initiatives. We're sorry it took so long.

If a historical perspective is an evaluative tool, let us see what we have learned. We learn from history that change does not happen precisely at that point where one changes the rules. At the height of our rejoicing are sown the seeds of our discontent. It is naïve to imagine that the differences we now experience will somehow stay the same, that if we could only get used to the way things are, we at least wouldn't have to endure that awful rupture again. Obsolescence stalks the contemporary composer's every song. If relevance is a criterion, then we must face the fact that our own favorite song, popular now, will soon be obsolete. Built into our very acceptance of a song must be an ability to let it go. Perhaps this is the time to thank all those composers in the vanguard of modern church music who, in this throwaway century, may already be out of date, those psalm, hymn, and song writers who prepared the way and bravely bore the awful burden of being first. We learn from history that there is always a painful struggle on the edge of something new, that as one musical style is flourishing, another style is dying and still another is being born. If we grasp that principle of overlapping, we can take comfort knowing that the world does not shift its position overnight. We will have time for adjustment, if only we can discern the future early on. But we miss vital clues because we fight them. We always react too quickly, and we usually react too hard, react to a reaction, solidify our opinion, and firmly shut the door. To cope with change means to face it squarely on the level of our feelings. History tells us to take time: time to listen, time to question, time to argue and to reject. Agents of change, remember when criticism comes hard and fast, when your back is to the wall, that this is gestation time. Opposition is an unavoidable phase. History tells us that time will tell if an idea was valid after all. What we need to do is survive the waiting with humor and with grace.

History shows that movements challenge institutions when the latter become impersonal and make unreasonable demands, that movements also become institutions, succumbing to the tendency to build three tents and settle, giving rise to newer movements to challenge the status quo. Movements ask, "Why? Why not?" Institutions answer with how-to's. Movements are of short duration. Institutions never seem to die. Our own revolt against legality has been too soon forgotten. Do we remember that the vernacular hymns of the Reformation proclaimed a new age of freedom, affirming the creative impulse of people with a new and spirited song? Yet how many Protestant churches welcomed the folk-style music of the sixties with open minds? Even today, most congregations would be a whole lot happier if those modern songs would simply go away. It is easy through hindsight to recognize the intolerance of others. Yet we ourselves are quick to set conditions, to frown on innovation particularly when it is not our own, to react to the threat of anything that has not been done before. Although we would deny it with vehemence, we are all a bit like Pope John XXII who faced a similar situation in 1324. We too would decree that the church should wait until modern music loses its force in secular circles before accepting it as fit for worship. If you doubt that description, introduce into your service several popular secular songs. There are some that are deeply Christian. See if you pass the test.

We learn from history that the church is preoccupied with making and upholding rules. This is how it handles the age-old struggle of preserving what others protest. There is a tension in each generation between tradition and innovation, law and spirit, system and value, a tension between the old and the new that seems to focus in our song. Not that music is the issue. We will never solve the church music "problem" because the problem is not the song. The problem lies much deeper, often concerning questions and attitudes we simply will not face. Music hints at those underlying issues, sometimes bellows them out loud. It reveals thoughts and feelings, tells what is really happening, is often indiscreet. It takes a stand for what is valued and rarely counts the cost.

If you want to know the future, listen to current songs. Music has a power. It stimulates campaigns, pushes products, goads to action, gives minorities a momentum that could get out of hand. Music is a danger, if you have something to protect. Perhaps that is why so much energy has been expended to control its access to the worshiping mind. What an awesome responsibility, to condemn or to condone. Strangely enough, what one era banishes another seems to bless. Instrumental music, the principle of troping, polyphony, harmony, the vernacular hymn, the guitar—once looked upon in horror—all were eventually tolerated and finally embraced. Six hundred and some years later, Pope John XXIII threw open windows bolted by John XXII. Only six short decades separate caution against cultural freedoms from the sound of Ghanaian drums. Perhaps with such shifting standpoints one must be careful not to swing too far. Already the guitar is an institution, a symbol of all that is new. Already we might ask with good reason, how did the Latin of so many centuries disappear so fast?

Innovation means we run the risk of losing what we love, yet we rebuild on cherished values when our changes flow from a deep sense of prayer, a respect for origins, and a concern for the common

good. Contemporary changes presuppose, therefore, a radical change of heart. We must look to the
Lord for guidance and less to legislation and officially
established norms. We must speak instead of discretion, of what is appropriate, of taste. It is time to trust
the Spirit who is capable of letting the young envision
the content of old people's dreams. It is time for
breaking open, time for extending welcome, time for
seeing through all those devices we have designed
for keeping out. We might look, for example, at our
hymnal. Do its covers say "amen" to the music
fortunate enough to be inside, automatically reject-
ing those inspired songs that postdate its publication
and all that will follow after? Can we develop a
loose-leaf attitude, one that cherishes its own special
heritage yet is ready to pop open and include other
riches with a certain amount of ease? History shows
that trusting the Spirit means people will make
mistakes. From time to time bad music and indiscre-
tions will slip into the service, and there will have to
be a purge. To err is to be human, yet it has always
been the Christian prerogative to be allowed to begin
again.

So here we are, beginning. A new day has
dawned. We are singing a brand-new song. "We
who love more than we can say, sing!" "We are
Easter people, and Alleluia is our song!" Our thanks
to Augustine whose optimism during negative times
continues to match our own. It is a grace to be living
at just this moment when the creative spirit no longer
finds itself on the windward side of locked cathedral
doors, when leadership reminds us that "music more
than any other resource makes a celebration of the
liturgy an attractive, human experience."[4] It is good

to be reminded to pay a little more attention to the human side of our experience with God. The motivation behind our singing is an offering to God, but the melodies are for us. We labor over our music not for God's sake but primarily for our own. Certainly God has a right to demand sincerity and dedication of our praise. That is why we must be selective, for the right choice of song can enable us to shed our clever defenses, bring us back again to our center, focus the moment collectively toward an uplifting of the heart. Only through a deeply human, deeply personal experience of the Word in community can we begin to really integrate our lives, let our praying persons through the medium of song spill over and beyond the borders of the service into the crevices of our day. Let song become a part of us. Let its message shape our actions. Song is especially helpful when it is biblically based and theologically sound. Previous emphasis on a "God up there," "above the clouds and starry skies," lulled the community into a strictly vertical thinking, diverting energy from a concern for this world and its many needs. Today our music must remind us of the God who came to share the stuff of our complicated lives, who came and will come again in justice and in peace. Our songs must help us prepare the way for that coming of the Lord.

It has been a long day's journey. Through the desert into the Promised Land, through the pre- and post-Temple periods, we marched with the children of Israel and marveled at their songs, marveled at the way they could articulate experience and link that to their Lord. We caught from early Christians a sensitivity to transcendence, singing: "Holy, holy,

holy, is the Lord God Almighty, who was and is and is to come!" (Rev. 4:8). Up, out of the catacombs and into the institutional church, we sang and then were silent as the unfolding forms of music revealed the splendor of their sound. Now we take our turn again at singing, take responsibility for writing our own songs, not in slavish imitation of former times, but by striving to match mood and meaning through contemporary means. We live our lives in relationship to all that has gone before, juxtapose word and Word in the Spirit with themes of here and now, grateful to the First Testament people for showing us how to be ourselves, grateful for a sense of the sacred inherited from the apostolic church, grateful to be able to address Yahweh as Father and Jesus the Christ as Lord. History's Inspiration joins with ongoing inspiration as we link human to transcendent and articulate the living Word in the accents of today. We stand at a point in history when the church has been reborn. A third testament is unfolding through the Spirit's inspiration as the incarnate Word takes flesh again in the story of our times. This is the contemporary challenge: to communicate that Word with dynamism as we make celebration moments of the turning points of life. Our songs must have meaning, for the quality of our religious experience relates quite closely to the quality of our song. Paul's statement at Corinth still has an authentic ring for us: "I will pray with my spirit, but I will pray also with my mind; I will sing with my spirit, but I will sing also with my mind" (I Cor. 14:15). Sing with understanding, sing a suitable song! The community is best served by songs that speak with a universal "I." Such songs can be claimed by everyone. They reflect a personal quality in a universal way. Setting the tone with Scripture, they express life's themes in general. We fill in the blanks with specifics, all of us, one by one.

Those who find it hard to pray might do well to begin with song. Those who find community difficult might join with several others in a sharing of that song. Song is God at work within us. "The Lord is my strength and my song" (Ps. 118:14). Music was perhaps the first bridge across that awful chasm created by the Reformation. Song linked many denominations in the bond of the Spirit long before they realized that the walls separating them from one another were already coming down. A clear sign that contemporary song is of the Spirit is its capacity to heal wounds and foster fellowship, to provide a means of communication when words fail before the pain of the past. The new songs are not denominational songs. They do not belong to one group more than to any other, but they are universally claimed because the word of God belongs to none exclusively, but to all. Relate this to your congregations. Tell them to open wide the windows of their hearts. The Word in song has a potential for prayer beyond all imagining. Let the singing soul and spirit prepare the way of the Lord.

4

COME AND SEE!

The world as we have known it is dying. More devastating than any act of God is the shattering of a strong symbolic sense through cumulative acts of people. Our once invulnerable institutions have already begun to crumble: democracy as a symbol of equal opportunity, woman as a symbol of submission, the Western world as a symbol of unchallenged supremacy, the church as a symbol of a stability unruffled by the trauma of change. Our symbols no longer communicate, says Rollo May, because we are caught in the crevice between times, when one age is relinquishing its hold on life and another is not yet born.[1] Many contemporary thinkers concur. We are trapped in a tenuous vacuum, suffering from what Carl Jung calls "a starvation of symbols" that normally feed us the meaning of life.

To some symbols we say, good riddance. It is hard to let others go. Yet as age-old symbols disintegrate, so unfortunately does our sensitivity to symbols. We have lost an inner vision. We have forgotten how to look at life, preferring to entrust our intuition to computer readouts and gigantic mechanical forms. Technology has killed so many of our symbols. Yet ironically, that same technology is itself a symbol, an unmistakable representation of highly pragmatic, achievement-oriented, impersonal times. As symbols

110

slip beyond our grasp, psychologists and philoso-
phers, theologians and poets, artists and children,
tell us in a variety of ways that a sense of the symbolic
is something that we dare not do without.

I wonder if we have not known this all along as we
cling tenaciously, and somewhat irrationally, to a
touch of the absurd. It is the week before Christmas
in Anytown, USA. The news belts out its threat of an
energy crisis along with its reports of anything but
peace on earth. People are cautioned to be conservative, to save electricity, to hold back. Driving along
after sunset, one would expect to be swallowed in a
canyon of darkness. But no, street after street
surrenders its welcoming surprise of lights, ablaze,
not just inside the houses, but even outside. In fact,
lights are all over the houses and the environment as
well. Trees, bushes, lamps, fences—the whole world
is suddenly alive with light. Why this waste? The
money could have been saved and spent unnecessar-
ily in some other way. The energy could have been
used for more television. Why this ridiculous waste?
A symbol. It says to you and me and the whole
criticizing world that each luminous house has a set
of values out of step with the status quo. It says:
Welcome, Light of lights, bathe this house and family
with your illuminating presence. It says: Hey,
people, this is what we believe in, and by your lights
we can see that you believe it too. Let us make a chain
of lights long and wide and excessive enough to wrap
around the globe, so that perhaps tomorrow we can
effect what this chain of lights envisions: link hands
and hearts and resources in the name of the One
whom these lights symbolize, the eternal Light of the
world. If and when the energy crisis comes down to

some hard decisions, the last thing we should extinguish are the dancing lights at Christmas, even if only for one long hour, we hang out our glimmers of hope. I would rather sit huddled in darkness and light my house on the outside, because I light the house there for you. It says to you as you huddle in darkness, that we marginated, exploited people have the Lord of light in common, and in spite of every difficulty, we still admit belief. So I light my Christmas lights for you, and you light yours for me, reflecting a level of meaning that no amount of words could ever communicate as effectively and as deeply, summarizing all those fragments of Scripture in a way we won't forget: "The people that walked in darkness have seen a great light; on those who live in a land of deep shadow a light has shone. You have made their gladness greater, you have made their joy increase" (Isa. 9:1-2 JB). "That life was the light of [all people,] a light that shines in the dark, a light that darkness could not overpower. . . . The Word was the true light that enlightens all . . . and he was coming into the world . . . and the world did not know him" (John 1:4-10 JB). "You are the light of the world. . . . Your light must shine in the sight of [all people,] so that, seeing your good works, they may give the praise to your Father in heaven" (Matt. 5:14-16 JB). In times of intense pragmatism, we need to have our symbols. In times of deprivation, we need to dream our dreams.

Symbols

Symbols communicate meaning. They help us understand something about those mysteries we cannot comprehend. They are the best and often only way to touch the deeper levels of life. A symbol is representative, directing attention beyond itself. Although it differs from what it represents, it does participate in the meaning and the power of that to which it points. Objectively, there is the conventional meaning derived from nature, culture, or tradition. Subjectively, there is also an association with another reality similar to the first.

A ring is round, for example. As a circle, it has neither beginning nor end. Lovers exchange rings on their wedding day as a pledge of unending love. A ring is a symbol of marriage, of love, treasured, not for its monetary value, but for what it represents. A butterfly emerges from its restricting cocoon after undergoing a radical transformation to beauty, freedom, flight. Jesus passed through death to life, burst from the tomb to liberate and lift us all to immortality. The butterfly is a symbol of resurrection. Symbols are the best possible expression of inexpressible reality. A holy man of this century—I do not remember his name—said as he lay dying: "I feel like a schoolboy going home for the holiday." The symbol of a schoolboy—pressured, programmed, not quite free—and the image of a homecoming, with all the warmth and welcome and delicious sense of deliverance that the symbol implies, is for me the most meaningful statement of death that I have yet to hear. I know what it feels like to come home for Christmas after a long, long time away; to return to my roots, to love, to belonging. I know what it means to die. Symbols are shared insights that tell us what life means. Christmas lights insist that a sense of celebration has a place in impoverished times. They remind us that love warms a wintering world, that grace is not always practical, that if God had obeyed popular predictions, Jesus would never have come.

Signs differ from symbols. They do not deal with insights, therefore they do not participate in the meaning of that to which they point. They are arbitrary and abstract. There is no emotional investment in a sign that exists as a natural consequence or a reality that has been arranged. Conventional signs of mathematics or music do not reveal new levels of meaning but are there to instruct and inform. There is prior agreement to what signs signify. A red light tells us to stop, and a green light tells us to go. Applause in our culture is a sign of approval. In another culture, people might show their approval by snapping their fingers or stamping their feet. A catcher's signs in baseball change from day to day. Words are signs, arbitrary arrangements of articulate sound that result in a thousand different ways to say "I love you" according to the language used.

Some words become more than signs. Some words are perceived as symbols. In post-Vietnam America, the hawk (bird of prey) and dove (bird of peace) symbolize two basic attitudes toward war. Watergate was once just a place to live, but in the traumatic seventies, a powerful symbol was born, communicating volumes of meaning to all who lived through that painful period. Auschwitz and Dachau are no longer just locations on a map, but symbols of such insanity that to recall them is to cry. For the believing Christian, a cross can never again be just a piece of wood. We do not create a symbol. It emerges from a series of circumstances, born of the "collective unconscious," and no amount of criticism has the power to kill it. Symbolic power continues until the situation that gave rise to it ceases to exist or the people who experienced it no longer remember, and the symbol has nothing more to say. Symbols are born and die. Signs are invented and removed.[2]

Our symbols are the way we look at life, our interpretation of what is real. Symbolism is important to religion as an access to ultimate reality. Our exposure to this world's meaning tells us something of the holy, reveals the One who warms like fire, sustains life like the sun, cleanses like water, holds us in integral relation like the branches on a tree. Fire, sun, living water, vine—these are recognized symbols of God. Just as beauty is born of the beholder, so the sensitive soul sees in creation potential symbols of its Creator. If we look and look, we are bound to see, to penetrate surface realities down to the very core of life, to develop a Christocentric eye that is quick to perceive love incarnate and delights in discovering that "at every turn life links us to the Lord" (Rom. 14:8 Phillips). The things we see will reveal to us realities we cannot see: daybreak, symbol of new beginnings, dawn after a long, dark night; spring promising a season of rebirth to the barren but believing heart.

We do not celebrate our symbols in isolation. Received from a group, they are shared by a group. In fact, we prefer to be with those who view the world as we do. That is why it is so hard to change from one religion to another or to leave a particular community or to relinquish one's citizenship. It is so hard that some people even hate to travel. They might tolerate a change of scenery, but they cannot cope with a shift in meaning. Not many people are cross-culturally comfortable, able to pass over to another symbolic base and return to their own enriched, able to grow through an appreciation of various approaches to life.

Scripture is full of symbolism. Both Testaments turn to symbolic language to communicate the incommunicable, to introduce the sacred through secular settings and events. The psalms remind me that I am "like a tree planted near running water" (Ps. 1:3 NAB), and, "as a doe longs for flowing streams" (42:1 JB), so I long for the Lord who is "my rock, and my fortress" (18:2), "my shepherd" (23:1), "a sun and shield" (84:11), who will "conceal me under the cover of his tent" (27:5), for "as the mountains are round about Jerusalem, so the Lord is round about his people" (125:2). Our faith rests on a solid base of signs and symbols. The rainbow, sign of God's covenant with us, is a symbol rich with associations. The ark too is a symbol—of deliverance from destruction, of brand-new beginnings all over the earth.

Jesus worked many signs and wonders during his short, significant ministry. He refused to reduce his miracles to the level of cheap magic, and he rebuked the scribes and Pharisees for their inability to interpret the signs of the times, giving them only the cryptic sign of Jonah, a strong resurrection symbol, in response to their demand for a sign. Jesus was so at home with symbolism that his words were two-edged swords barely pricking consciousness yet capable of piercing the heart. He spoke of being born again, but Nicodemus dismissed the notion as naturally naïve. Jesus offered living water to the woman at the well, but she doubted because he had no bucket, and the well was very deep. Even his disciples failed to realize that he linked flesh to spirit in his metaphors of life. They were puzzled by the parable of the sower until he gave the clue to its meaning, that the seed was in fact the word of God rejected or received. When Jesus said, "I have food to eat that you do not know about," the disciples wondered, "Has someone been bringing him food?"—not knowing that the food he meant was the Father's sustaining will (John 4:32-4). When he offered his flesh and blood as source of life, many walked with him no more.

Jesus himself was the fulfillment of an earlier prophetic symbol: "There shall come forth a shoot from the stump of Jesse, and a branch shall grow out of his roots. And the Spirit of the Lord shall rest upon him" (Isa. 11:1-2). Jesus referred to himself as door, bread, living water, light, shepherd, cornerstone, vine that relates to us as branches. Taken literally, these statements are absurd. I am a person, not a twig; yet in relation to God I am indeed like a branch that extends from the tree of life. Jesus is like a door offering access to the Father. He is like bread to starving spirits, like water that touches thirst and transforms it, like a shepherd concerned for his flock. Each image reveals another dimension of the One so hard to know, gives us a hint of that Kingdom and what it takes to bring it about. We are sent out like lambs among wolves, exposed and vulnerable in the face of violence and values that differ from ours. We are to be like leaven, an influence that uplifts. Sheep and goats, weeds and wheat, wine and wineskins, the seed and the sower, light beneath a bushel, salt of the earth, plants planted by the Father, keys of the Kingdom, lilies of the field: the Christian message is steeped in symbolism. Perhaps that is why it continues to be so hard for us to grasp. We do not know how to handle parables. We prefer the cold, hard facts. Some of us even think fairy tales are silly and mock imaginary friends. We are just too literal to encounter what is real.

The seed of Christianity fell on symbolic soil and the emerging church burgeoned with symbolism that permeated its writing, its music, its art. The letters of Paul include passages of pure poetry with insights still full of meaning. The church is the extension of Christ's body, says Paul, needing hand, eye, every single member in order to function properly. It is all of that and more. "Do you not know that you are God's temple and that God's Spirit dwells in you?" (I Cor. 3:16). Indeed we are a letter from Christ "written not with ink but with the Spirit of the living God, not on tablets of stone but on tablets of human hearts" (II Cor. 3:3). We are secure yet vulnerable, for "we who have this spiritual treasure are like common clay pots, in order to show that the supreme power belongs to God, not to us" (4:7 TEV). The book of Revelation is a symbol from end to end, concealing its meaning behind a splash of images: winged creatures, the sea of glass, the scroll, the Lamb, the seven seals, the four horsemen, the woman with child, the beast, the marriage feast, the new Jerusalem, the book of life. The rich, symbolic word of Scripture invites serious scrutiny. Like the jar of oil, it pours out its meaning without ever running dry, reveals yet conceals its secret to insure that we will probe again. The early church, born beneath

118

tongues of fire, caught that symbolic spirit and fashioned a tradition of words rich with imagery and meaning. Ignatius of Antioch, marked for martyrdom at the turn of the first century, wrote to the church of Rome: "I am God's wheat, I am ground by the teeth of wild beasts that I may end as the pure bread of Christ." The church, referred to as Christ's Body, was also called his bride. At times it was a ship on stormy seas en route to a haven of peace. Members were sealed with the sign of the cross, earned the palm of martyrdom which guaranteed the crown of eternal life. Their symbols of the Holy included the all-seeing eye of the Father; the hand of God from Old Testament imagery; a fish (*ichthus*—third-century acrostic for Jesus Christ, Son of God, Savior); the *Chi Rho* (derived from the first two letters of the Greek *Christos*). During the peak of the persecution, signs, symbols, and catacomb secrecy created a communications code for fugitives in the faith.

Today we have the sacraments, signs full of symbolism, to link us with our past. Yet our sensitivity to these symbols has been severely damaged because their association to life as we know it has been severed. How did we get so stale? We killed some symbols out of fear, fear that we would one day find ourselves bowed down before a golden calf, fear that our visual representations would replace the One we worship. Of course, there is always the danger that our symbols of ultimate reality might get out of hand, that we might love too much our carbon copies and dismiss the original as unreal. We are quite prone to idols, to misusing and abusing the things of God. We are also prone to

119

misinterpretation from those who are quick to cry idolatry when that is not the case at all. A lot of beautiful art was destroyed on a premise that had no foundation in fact. Icons, statues, stained-glass windows, paintings—all of these at one time or another fanned the flames of fear. Other symbols died because of our apathy. We really did not care to keep them because they were representative of another time and place. Symbols that fail to communicate are simply souvenirs. We can only inherit symbols when we affirm the whole situation to which those symbols spoke. We lost a sense of symbolism because we held onto some symbols too long. We thought by holding on to them we were holding on to truth. When we saw that they were meaningless, for one wild moment we wondered if what they stood for was also dead. Caught in a kind of idolatry that put systems between ourselves and truth, we threw away our images in disgust, forgetting that truth must be sought anew in every age, that each generation is called upon to interpret the signs of its own times.

We are a little wiser now. We know what we must do. The problem we face is how to restore a reverence, how to recapture a relationship that has changed with the changing times. For years we manipulated creation to meet our so-called needs. We blemished the face of the earth with our cities, scarred its beauty, sucked its oil, ransacked its riches, gouged its gems. We have no use for mystery. Secrets insult our genius. The elements have nothing to say to us because we no longer listen to wind, rivers, rain. These are just things to be calibrated to determine how much interference they will give to what we invent. Stars remind us we still have some steel cluttering up the landscape of Mars. We reminisce about growing things as we thaw our packaged food. We lost our symbols when we lost a reality we once took for granted. Until we value again the stuff of poetry, the world we inhabit will be a shell we carefully rearrange. As long as we send Valentines, as long as we dare to dance in the streets when our team takes the Stanley Cup, and celebrate *HOCKEY* inaugurations with parties and parades, we have a ray of hope. But if we insist on moving national holidays to suit our own convenience, forgetting about feasts and creating long weekends for tennis and for golf, we hover dangerously close to the edge of no return. The rhythm of feasts and seasons, the liturgy of the universe, is the siren that will save us from our utilitarian selves. We long to tell our stories through a rebirth of myth and symbol in a new spiritual language that is rich enough to captivate and wiser than we are. We live in that time between times, a time of trial and error, a tense time of transition, a time of beginning again. Let us make the best of this second chance. The Word speaks through parables and symbols in the present as well as the past. It is our responsibility to select the raw materials that will best express this truth. The Way winds along the path of tradition. We follow the footsteps before us but wear a brand-new pair of shoes.

In *The Protestant Era,* Paul Tillich laments the loss of sacramental (symbolic) thinking in the churches. Revolt against the institutions of the medieval church led Protestantism to reject symbolic forms as a deterrent to the soul's direct communion with God. In the wake of twentieth-century reform, many are

121

reconsidering that initial, unbending stance. Tillich insists that all of life is a potential resource for worship, for everything rises from that Ground of Being which is its ultimate source.[3] Dietrich Bonhoeffer speaks of God as "the 'beyond' in the midst of our life . . . not on the borders of life but at its center."[4] We must learn to harness the senses to assist and enhance the contemplative stirrings of the heart.

We are lovers of beauty and ardent admirers of art, moved by color and conditioned by form. When did we first begin to suspect that such grandeur might not be of God? Why are our homes and party places so alive with the best our creativity has to offer and our "sacred spaces" so devoid of that which we secretly love? What is the sin of stained glass and sculpture or the scandal of an "alleluia" tossing rainbow colors from a banner or a mural or even, God forgive me, from calligraphy painted boldly on the wall? Haven't those very churches told us that God looked upon creation and saw, before our filters and our censors, that all of it was good? Our God deals with images. We ourselves are copies created "in the image of God" (Gen. 1:27) and reflect, along with all of creation, eternal attributes. While we await a rebirth of images and a more mature sense of the sacred in our celebration of life and Word, let us whisper a prayer of gratitude for Michelangelo, that nonconformist, for monks who illustrated manuscripts, for anonymous painters of icons, for Christian catacomb dwellers who paused to doodle on stone, for all those pioneers of graphic beauty whose gift received no recompense, whom contemporary artists imitate and greeting cards exploit. We who witness a dynamic revival of liturgical art in this century must remember that artists do not create new symbols, that designs on banners, book jackets, and posters, if they are truly symbolic, simply depict those symbols to which we have already given assent. At present, industrial trademarks and logos are stealing the symbolic scene as commercial genius dangles universals to activate our basic needs. If we were to take a survey, I wonder what the children of this generation would list as "the real thing"?

As Protestants seek to rediscover symbols, Catholics struggle to renew them. Together we must ascertain which of those biblical values that shape our behavior lend themselves to symbolic form. Some ancient symbols still limp with life. Others must be quietly interred. Our feelings give rise to many more fantasies than we dare admit out loud or would grant tangible existence outside our imagining selves. Symbols are concretized feelings. They presume an emotional, wholehearted response, a publication of personal belief. A pledge to live symbolically would force us to shed a little of our timidity and reserve. We would have to become more playful, come out in support of celebration, weave some wasteful patterns through the routines we observe. We would have to come to terms with faith, tap into our feelings, decide what an occasion means.

Can we name some surviving symbols? The Advent wreath is one. It is more than a decoration, although its four candles in a setting of greens is decorative enough. The wreath represents an attitude of silent, reflective vigilance until salvation comes. It tells us that Christmas is more than a commemoration of a birthday long, long past. The feast is an annual reminder that Christ comes again and again in spirit to the open, inviting heart, before coming with finality in glory at the end. So we light candles in expectation and quietly prepare. Rekindle the fire of our love, we pray. Come, Lord Jesus, come! The Advent wreath is a symbol of all who wait for God. The Christmas tree is a symbol that represents more than warm memories of home, far more than a flash of tinsel under which we tuck our gifts. In the Garden stood the tree of knowledge, symbol of perfection, symbol of our sin. The One we welcome at Christmas came to redeem us on the tree of the cross. "I am the vine, you are the branches" (John 15:5). At Christmas we remember and celebrate salvation symbolized by a tree as we and "all the trees of the wood sing for joy before the Lord, [who] comes" (Ps. 96:12-13). Let us trim our tree religiously and pray with each decoration that joy, hope, liberation, and peace might ornament the earth through Christ's coming through the coming year. The tree itself should symbolize our hope for a better world, as it guards the gifts we give to those near to us, symbols of the gift of God we would share generously with all.

We invest our symbols with meaning. They in turn enrich our lives with new meaning and deepen our wavering faith. The ashes we receive on Ash Wednesday remind us of our critically close association with banality. We are indeed of dust and to dust we shall return. So many of our undertakings leave a residue of ash. We bear a responsibility for what we have done to the earth, our mother, for environmental atrocities. In Lent we purge ourselves of evil tendencies and burn away our guilt. One Ash

Wednesday evening, we gathered in our chapel on Pine Road, a rather unlikely mix of parents, children, Sisters, priests, residents of The Bridge, a live-in community for teen-agers once hooked on alcohol or drugs. One by one, we threw into a fiery brazier some representation of an evil that had control of us. A photograph, a clipping, a headline, a memento—we tossed them to the flames. A picture of some gourmet food. For unnecessary opulence while others starve: Lord, have mercy. A love letter. For letting him father my illegitimate child: Lord, have mercy. A wrinkled piece of paper. For new year resolutions never kept: Lord, have mercy. A picture of a syringe. For this demon drug that destroyed me, my family, my home: Lord, have mercy. Forgive us our trespasses. Lead us not into temptation. Deliver us from evil. We wore those ashes boldly, branded by our sins, believing that the strength of the crucified Christ would saturate that symbol and set our senses free. That Easter, we began again, newly alive and hopeful in the Lord who conquered sin.

Our symbols have an uncanny capacity to effect what they signify through the power of inspiration. Total immersion at baptism is a graphic statement that we pass from bondage to a new mode of being and emerge born again. A symbolic use of environment—Easter sunrise service on a hill, a reflection on Living Water beside a running stream—helps us integrate our senses around a given theme. The use of light and darkness, for example, is a simple yet effective symbol. During Advent or the Easter Vigil service or at a wake for one we love, we wait in a darkness that matches our mood and pray for acceptance and peace. Just the simple act then of lighting a candle is often enough to communicate exactly what we feel.

Suitable symbols assist our faith, bad symbols disrupt it. Mary symbols illustrate this point. The old-fashioned May crowning and procession is an ecumenical embarrassment today, commanding too much visibility for something so misunderstood. As the first Christian feminist, Mary is strikingly relevant to our times. She too risked everything by assenting to a role that had no precedence. She did not say, No woman has ever done this before, therefore it cannot be. Mary, a woman, was ordained from all eternity to present God to the world. Let our symbols communicate this. Similarly, the traditional manner of distributing communion has been restored to the Catholic liturgy for the value of its sign. We take and break the bread of peace. That is our Eucharist. A wafer that is not really bread, that is placed on the tongue and melts in the mouth, what does that signify? It is easier to assent to the presence of God than to admit that the wafer is bread! Weak symbols weaken faith. Strong symbols support it.

Catholicism has clung far too long to symbols that have died, symbols that fail to communicate because the collective unconscious no longer affirms their meaning. All the Christian churches today suffer an impoverishment of symbols, hang suspended between the loss of a tradition and new forms still to come. Last spring, I was in the South Pacific on the underside of the world, where seasons are the reverse of ours, but feast days stay the same. It was Easter in Christchurch, New Zealand. My past had prepared me for a season of rebirth. The thaw of a frozen landscape, the return of birds and flowers, longer days promising long, lazy summer days ahead, a "good to be alive" feeling that accompanies Resurrection in the spring—such was my expectation. But this was Easter in Christchurch, and it wasn't exactly spring. Summer vacation had just ended, and children were dragging reluctant feet to school. The leaves were turning crimson. The clouds were dark and threatening, and the day was biting cold. We were midway into autumn. Spring symbols made no sense. The church, the liturgy, the century—all was the same as in Philadelphia, but everything had changed. It was a season for passing over, a time to test for symbols—not new life, but fulfillment, not seeds sown, but a harvest, not beginnings, but fruition—a looking forward by looking back. There was potential for rich imagery here, if only the church would acknowledge the need and the culture give assent. We must become more sensitive to environmental differences, be universally appropriate, universally relevant, not universally the same. We have taken some fine first steps. The U. S. Catholic Bishops' Committee on the Liturgy released a sensitive statement back in 1972. I wonder how many have read it.

People in love make signs of love, not only to express their love but also to deepen it. Love never expressed dies. Christians' love for Christ and for each other, Christians' faith in Christ and in each other, must be expressed in the signs and symbols of celebration or it will die. The signs and symbols of worship can give bodily expression to faith as we celebrate. Faith grows when it is well expressed in celebration. Good celebrations foster and nourish faith. Poor celebrations weaken and destroy faith.[5]

Good celebrations demand meaningful ritual. Ritual

is simply the acting out of our commitment to symbols and myths.

Ritual

Ever since Adam and Eve were banished from the garden of ease and told to make it on their own ingenuity, human behavior has been ritually arranged around those basic activities of gathering and preparing food, securing shelter, rearing children, appeasing the deity, and death. Every nation, tribe, and family patterns these activities in its own unique way. Added to that behavior organized toward purely practical ends is a great deal of movement and exchange that has no apparent purpose. These useless, wasteful gestures are actually extremely significant in binding the group together. We call them celebrations. They make meaning out of life. To celebrate is human, a gift from a God who playfully arranged our environment and cast us in a leading role. We communicate best when we celebrate. We are, in fact, ritual makers, "always trying to write the best of our lives with each other into some kind of shorthand of word and gesture."[6] The celebration of birth and belonging; departure and homecoming; growth, depth, and dying is authentic religious ritual when it comes to grips with the human struggle in order to transform it. In this sense, religious ritual is redemptive. Whether our rites are strong or sterile is strictly up to us.

Ritual surrounds us. The way we face the morning; greet one another with a hug or a handshake; conform to codes of behavior at weddings, funerals, and graduations; observe social etiquette, Olympic

pageantry, baseball's seventh inning stretch; even to
the way we comb our hair, we are rigidly routine.
Why then are we down on religious ritual? Perhaps
because we have experienced so much bad ritual—
ritual that has ceased to evolve with culture, ritual
that is dull and boring, manipulative or immature.
Even those churches that claim no obvious ritual are
in fact ritually bound. Consider the pattern of most
services, call to worship at the beginning, benediction at the end, the interspersing of scripture,
sermon, song, the routine procedures in starting a
hymn, taking up the offering, conducting the
Communion service, determining the appropriate
moments when the congregation will sit or stand. We
should examine our ritual patterns, evaluate their
effectiveness, decide which actions are helpful and
which ones ought to change. Authentic ritual roots in
human experience to integrate and renew us. Such
ritual thrives at the Rose Bowl where the roar of the
crowd matches the excitement of pageantry and
parade, where it is OK to cheer the winner, where
thousands respond as one. We are most ourselves in
secular settings where bursts of genuine feeling
sweep away our mask. In the presence of the One
who made us, however, and knows us as we are,
crippling inhibitions alter the way we normally act.
The use of our body in religious ritual is often in
opposition to our basic human response. Happy or
sad, enthused or bruised, we set our faces, modulate
our voices, and on cue, all together, kneel, sit, stand.
Our churches promote segregation, separating experience from its expression, our feelings from our
faith. No wonder we run from those robot roles,
escape to the theater, amusement park, stadium, or

circus to be wholehearted participants in the merry-go-round of life. When we are happy, we let go—laugh, skip, twirl, dance—anywhere but in church.

Consider the rationale that confines us to our places, conditioning us to prefer a cerebral worship to a total human response. That puritanical paralysis that afflicts the Western world is not based on biblical fact. "Praise [God] with drums and dancing," cries the psalmist (Ps. 150:4 TEV), "let them dance in praise of [God's] name" (149:3 JB). And remember, as they welcomed liberation, the women of Israel danced.

Creation is a movement: and the sacred dance arises from the need to identify with the eternal round of the creative forces in the cosmos. . . . The whole of existence is woven into the cycle of becoming, stretching between birth and death, experiencing ascent and decline; and life, when it has clothed itself for a while with sounds, gestures, forms, when it has ruled a while in manifestations, returns in silence to its own slumber.[7]

Saturday morning in Jerusalem, small circles of Yemenite Jews dance before the Western Wall. At times they hold the scrolls aloft and the exuberance of their movements spills over in sheer, contagious joy. Once again David is dancing in delight before his God, a foolish gesture in the eyes of those not childlike in their praise. Hands and feet are restless to join the heart that leaps in love. A glance at the history of religions shows that ritual movement is integral to very many worship rites in cultures around the world: Yoga positions, Islamic prayer postures, dances for rain or sun, warriors or the harvest, of Shakers and Ashantis, Krishna and Shiva, to name just a few.

And just as he who dances with his body, rushing through the rotating movement of the limbs, acquires the right to share in the round dance, in the same way he who dances the spiritual dance, always moving in the ecstasy of faith, acquires a right to dance in the ring of all creation.
—Ambrose, fourth-century Bishop of Milan[8]

Medieval monastic orders used ritual dance to foreshadow eternal dancing. "Blessed in soothe is that dance whose company is infinity, whose circling is eternity, whose song is bliss" (Bonaventure, *ca.* 1260).[9] After centuries of sitting still, we are starting to creep cautiously out of our stiff shells. If only we could erase the stereotype of someone somersaulting up the aisle. Ritual movement has many dimensions, some especially suited to an awkward, arthritic faith. The smallest gesture, done with meaning, is part of the ritual dance. "So use your bodies for God's glory" (I Cor. 6:20 TEV). We lift our hands, bow our heads, follow in procession. Why, we are already dancing!

Perhaps the critical issue underlying sterile ritual is our perception of the transcendent. If we relate to God as an abstraction, impersonal worship structures will follow. If God is experienced as a presence that is meaningful and active in our life, we will be more inclined to relate through worship that is dynamic and wholly human. The question of religious ritual then becomes a question of relationship that brings us back to prayer. So the circle closes. Prayer, inseparable from life, a savoring of life, gifts, God, a reshaping of life when it fails to conform to fundamental standards of justice, this kind of prayer

131

determines the ritual that is our link to the transcendent, lifting the heart beyond its absorption in time into a timelessness, not through programmed actions only, but a free use of the gifts of the earth shared through the priesthood of all believers, where everyone participates in the worship experience according to personal gift. Like a dance, it comes back to the individual rich with creative potential in the creating Spirit who dwells within.

What each one has to give is precisely what the community needs to have. The task is to determine the nature of our gift and then proceed to release it. We waste far too much energy coveting someone else's talent. We cheat ourselves with comparisons. What good would it be if all in the community were preachers or musicians or artists? We would soon miss the janitor, the one who makes the coffee, and all those quiet workers behind the scenes. "Give, and it shall be given to you . . . pressed down, shaken together, running over" (Luke 6:38). The very act of giving prompts a giving in return. To give our gift is costly. It means that we can never again be the mystery that we were. It means that by sheer effort we will have to dig up that talent—if we can remember where we hid it. We will have to bust that bushel basket and let our person sparkle, not for our own advantage, but for the glory of the Father. It means opting for inconvenience. The knock on the door will always come when we would rather be in bed. Our ritual today needs every kind of talent to relate our prayer to life. We are the ones capable of discerning life's primary rhythms, the things that move, uplift, inspire. What an awesome responsibility for any worshiping community, to insure that its

religious ritual is rooted in life and thereby authenti-
cally real.

Symbolism reveals dimensions of meaning in
day-to-day routine. Ritual combines that catalog of
symbols in a dramatic commentary, investing values
with a force that enables mere mortals to commune
with God. There is a fine line between religious ritual
and performance. Any course of training for the
congregation must make that distinction clear. If we
start with and stress personal prayer, there will be
less danger of gimmick or inclination to fad. A
healthy religious ritual always has room for surprise.
In fact, surprise is expected, for shades of meaning
surface in celebration that eluded the planning stage.
That is because we are "serendipitous . . . always
finding things we are not looking for." Eugene
Kennedy continues his description of healthy religious ritual that contributes to psychological balance.

People may be struck at this moment by one aspect of the
ritual, while tomorrow they may respond to some other
part of it. We abandon rituals that fail to make room for our
distractibility or that are so impoverished we can never
find anything new in them. . . . Religious needs in human
beings are deep and it takes a great deal of human
understanding to sense and express them with a ritual that
will make us feel at home with ourselves and with God.[10]

Secular society is always producing to meet this
neglected need. The success of large-scale catastrophe films is a fascinating phenomenon. *Jaws, King
Kong, Exorcist, Earthquake,* and similar flights of fancy
tap into that vulnerability beneath our cocky veneer.
Long ago we bit into that apple in a spree of "let's
pretend." Today we are still insisting that our

scientific genius has everything under control. We have conquered the mysteries of earth and space. There is nothing left to fear. Let's pretend we are omnipotent and ignore the unleashed fury lurking deep in the bowels of the earth. But beneath this public bravado lies the whimper of a frightened child. For want of a place to run to, we are drawn to make-believe horrors with which our fears can identify, where to cower is not cowardly, where reality is unreal. We come away grateful to be alive and safe and able to pretend again. Healthy ritual lets us admit that indeed we are not gods, incorporates feelings of fear and frustration as a preliminary to grace. Genuine catharsis comes not with *Jaws* but through Jesus, who meets all our anxiety with a comforting, "Do not be afraid" (Luke 12:32 TEV).

We are carnal people. Our faith cries out from experience for some clear, unmistakable sign, to touch and be touched, know and be known, through the avenues of our senses. For us, seeing is believing. God, loving Father, who made us in this manner, sent us the perfect image of infinity in nonthreatening, finite form, the clearest, least cluttered Word. "The goodness and loving kindness of God our Savior appeared" (Titus 3:4), "made visible in the flesh" (I Tim. 3:16 JB), to lead us from things seen to things unseen, from the visible to the invisible, from flesh to spirit. "We have seen his glory" (John 1:14), the prologue to the Fourth Gospel proclaims as the Word takes human flesh. "We have seen the Lord!" (20:25), the disciples tell Thomas, after that same flesh died and rose again in defiance of nature's law. "Whoever sees me, sees the one who sent me" (12:45), said Jesus, and early in his ministry, he

extended an invitation to all to "come and see!"
(1:39). Consequently, many "saw what Jesus did,
and they believed in him" (11:45 TEV). And that
other disciple, when he approached the empty tomb,
"saw and he believed" (20:9 JB). We Christians
cannot easily dismiss this sensual dimension of faith.
God took a very visual approach in securing our
salvation, making certain that "we have seen with
our own eyes; that we have watched and touched
with our hands: the Word, who is life" (I John 1:1 JB),
that we might more readily believe. Yet seeing is only
the beginning, for faith derived from things seen and
nothing more is not even faith. "Hope that is seen is
not hope. For who hopes for something [one] sees?
But if we hope for what we do not see, we wait for it
with patience" (Rom. 8:24b-25 TEV). We await a
breakthrough to meaning as "we fix our attention,
not on things that are seen, but on things that are
unseen. What can be seen lasts only for a time but
what cannot be seen lasts forever" (II Cor. 4:18).

Our physical eye is a window watching for deeper
things, sight leading to insight through the spiritual
eye of faith. Teilhard de Chardin approached all of
creation with reverence, recognizing religious ritual
in the liturgy of life.

I worship a God who can be touched, and I do indeed
touch him, this God of mine, over the whole surface and
deep down in the depths of that matter which confines me:
but to take hold of him as I would wish (simply in order not
to stop touching him), I must never rest in anything. I must
go always on and on through and beyond each partial
achievement, borne onwards at each moment by creatures
and at each moment go beyond them, in an endless
welcoming of them and separation from them.[11]

135

With love, then, we embrace the universe as symbol of the holy, never wholly surrendering to any temporal beatitude, grateful for every assist from our senses, more grateful for the spiritual sense that perceives truth and unmasks it. "Happy are those who have not seen and yet believe" (John 20:29). This is the insight we seek as we encounter visual reminders, the vision we envision as we cry out: "I want to see" (Mark 10:51 NAB).

We reach then toward a ritual that is neither too human nor too impersonal, one that is meaningful enough to take us beyond ourselves. A search for meaning is a search for wholeness, for ourselves, our community, the world. No other prayer is valid in a world wallowing in so much need. Concern for others is the pivotal point between selfish or selfless structure. It drives us to lift the Word from pages and wrap it again in flesh. As that gentle Jewish mystic, Rabbi Abraham Heschel, said shortly before he died, "Remember that life is a celebration." Let us make our feasts celebrations then and not solemnities, so that our lives will be less sombre, so that we "tremble with excitement," can "see this and be filled with joy" (Isa. 60:5). As we learn to live symbolically, we will discover metaphors of the eternal in all that we see and touch. As "ministers of a new covenant, not in a written code but in the Spirit; for the written code kills, but the Spirit gives life" (II Cor. 3:6), we dare indeed to be "doers of the word, and not hearers only" (James 1:22).

> now the ears of my ears awake and
> now the eyes of my eyes are opened[12]

5

DOERS OF THE WORD

Poverty. Hunger. Drought. Disease. Hatred. Oppression. The blue-green globe, beneficiary of peace and goodwill, drifts through the shimmering galaxy, stained with war and scarred by catastrophe. Floods, famine, and furious upheavals increase and multiply along with its people. Borders between nations are sketched, erased, and arbitrarily rewritten with violence and blood. Hovels house those made in the image and likeness of God. Desperate fingers scratch dry dust for any living thing. The land, so long dominated, is seeking its revenge. Empty wells, ruined crops, glacier cold in tropical meridians, the paucity of natural resources in relation to the immense demand, tell us in no uncertain terms: we are but caretakers of the earth, not its master. What right have we to determine economic wealth and economic ruin, to formulate policies that indicate who will live and who will die?

Looking through lace curtains on a hard-earned patch of green, where there is freedom of choice, and opportunity abounds, grim facts seem merely statistics for some vague and future terror on some dim and distant day. It does not seem to matter that 6 percent of the present world community consumes more than one-third of its food resources, overeating

137

while others starve. We are unaware—or uncon-cerned—that five hundred million hungry people dream, not of success or a two-car garage, but of enough bread to make it through another brutal day. The pointed shards of those shattered dreams stab at our indifference today, and must, until we bleed.

Deprivation, hunger, poverty, oppression, these are the weapons of war we face in the new millennium. These are the demons that mock the promise: "Peace I leave with you; my peace I give to you" (John 14:27), taunting, "Where is your God?" (Ps. 42:10). We who inherit the promise must also accept the responsibility for making that promise come true. If we want peace, we must make peace, for peace is something we do. Peace happens with every single gesture of goodwill. "If a brother or sister is ill-clad and in lack of daily food, and one of you says to them, 'Go in peace, be warmed and filled,' without giving them the things needed for the body, what does it profit? So faith by itself, if it has no works, is dead" (James 2:14-17). We can no longer turn deaf ears to the cry of the human family as we hasten to our comforts unscathed. "All you who pass this way, look and see" (Lam. 1:12 JB): the sorrow and uncertainty, the misery and injustice, the incredible want and the hardness of our hearts. "Alas for you!" Jesus cried—to all those who "do not practice what they preach" . . . who "tie up heavy burdens and lay them on [other's] shoulders" . . . "who shut up the kingdom of heaven in [people's] faces" (Matt. 23:3-4, 13 JB). Woe to all of us who hear the word of God and do not keep it! The time is coming, in fact it is already here, when we "will hear of wars and rumors of wars . . . nation will fight

138

DOERS OF THE WORD

against nation, and kingdom against kingdom. There will be famines and earthquakes here and there. All this is only the beginning of the birthpangs . . . with the increase of lawlessness, love in most [people] will grow cold" (24:6-8, 12 JB). In contrast to such devastation, the word of God weaves a counterpoint of good news. "The blind see again, and the lame walk, lepers are cleansed, the deaf hear, and the dead are raised to life." This marvelous alternative, this good news, "is proclaimed to the poor; and happy is the [one] who does not lose faith in me" (11:5-6 JB). These messianic miracles that accompanied Jesus will, must, continue to happen through us, for we have been empowered to do as he did, provided we hold tight to faith. "Truly, truly, I say to you . . . who believes in me will also do the works that I do; and greater works than these will [you] do" (John 14:12). Each of us is commissioned to "depart from evil, and do good; seek peace, and pursue it" (Ps. 34:14). Our faith must influence our behavior or we will pay the penalty for indifference and writhe with an affliction that will bring us to our knees. Even now we face captivity again, this time to the elements we thought we had tamed. "Hear, O earth; behold, I am bringing evil upon this people, the fruit of their devices, because they have not given heed to my words" (Jer. 6:19). We beg the land to yield an increase, the rivers to offer sweet water, the sun to warm our frozen limbs, the wind to withhold its anger. We listen for words of encouragement, for stark syllables of good news, to spur us on to action, as "doers of the word, and not hearers only," so that we might never be just a "hearer that forgets but a doer that acts" (James 1:22, 25).

The catalyst of hope in these traumatic times is the word of God, which existed "from the beginning, before earth came into being" (Prov. 8:23 JB), that word which "will stand for ever" (Isa. 40:8). Creative and creating, "by the word of the Lord the heavens were made, and all their host by the breath of [God's] mouth" (Ps. 33:6). Light, land, vegetation, animals, man and woman: God spoke all into being. God said: "Let there be . . . and there was . . . and it was good" (Gen. 1). In the prologue to the Fourth Gospel, we move from word to Word. Its opening phrase is identical to the first words of Genesis and is therefore a fitting introduction to God's word and work in the new dispensation. "In the beginning was the Word, and the Word was with God, and the Word was God" (John 1:1). This divine verbalization expressed itself in human terms. "The Word became flesh and dwelt among us, full of grace and truth" (v. 14). Jesus is, in the fullest sense, God's self-disclosure. To hear his word and accept it is to hear the word of God. He is the new creation in spirit and in truth, bringing to life life-giving powers in all who keep his word.

God's word is source of life. That word is also law. For the Jew, the totality of God's will is God's word as law. The criteria of fidelity: "I will delight in thy statutes; I will not forget thy word. . . . I will keep thy law" (Ps. 119:16, 44). For the Christian, Jesus summed up the new revelation with a new commandment that subjects us to a law of love. Its demands are hard upon us, to forfeit our lives, if necessary, "to live a life of love" (II John 6 JB). Both Testaments attest to the primacy of love, but differ in relationship to law.

God's word is prophetic oracle, overcoming all

opposition in its urgency to be heard: deaf ears, hardened hearts, hesitant messengers. At times it threatened destruction as punishment of infidelity. Then it would promise a blessing, spoken in tones of exquisite tenderness, to the loyal remnant of believers. The prophetic word is both a harsh and a gentle word, recalling a covenant commitment to those who have gone astray. Proclamation, preparation—this is the prophetic burden. In the prologue to Second Isaiah, the good news of God's coming is announced and the prophet is commissioned to "prepare the way of the Lord" (Isa. 40:3). Centuries later, that same passage is applied to John the Baptist, the last of the old prophetic tradition, the first to herald the new. "He went through the whole Jordan district proclaiming a baptism of repentance for the forgiveness of sins, as it is written in the book of the sayings of the prophet Isaiah: *A voice cries in the wilderness: Prepare a way for the Lord, make his paths straight*" (Luke 3:3-4 JB). Twenty centuries later, those words are addressed to us, extending the import of the message to every time and place. Outdistanced and outnumbered, we set out like wolves among sheep, snapping at the heels of a smug social order. Defiantly, the word howls down empty structures, reverberates against slack moral fiber, entices those who wander ever so slightly from precedent. Although but a voice in the wilderness, we can be heard preparing a way in the world for the Word. Faithful to its energetic character, the word of God involves us actively as we struggle to straighten paths, fill in gaps, remove barriers, smooth over rough edges, so that all the world might "see the salvation of God" (v. 6 JB).

141

God's word is activity. God's word *does*. It creates, commands, frees, accomplishes, heals, redeems. So we address the Word as Life, Lawgiver, Liberator, Prince of Peace, Healer, Redeemer. So too we bring life, fidelity, liberation, peace, healing, and redemption as we strive to do that Word. The Word is both verbal and verb, accomplishing what it intends. "The word that goes forth from my mouth does not return to me empty, without carrying out my will and succeeding in what it was sent to do" (Isa. 55:1 JB). God's word is a constant life-giving source, calling forth poetry from dryness, coaxing a fragile hope to emerge from physical and emotional ruin. As God does, so shall we do. This is the essence of the commandments. "The word is very near to you; it is in your mouth and in your heart, so that you can do it" (Deut. 30:14). Like the people of Israel, gathered in the shadow of Sinai, we cry out with sincerity: "All that the Lord has spoken we will do" (Exod. 19:8). This word is pronounced by a personal God who, through the Word, communicates with people one to one and expects a personal response. "My mother and my brothers are those who hear the word of God and do it" (Luke 8:21). The loving intimacy of a family relationship is promised to those who are doers of the word. And what is it that we must do? The prophet Micah sums up God's expectation in a phrase that deserves to be branded on our hearts. "This is what Yahweh asks of you: only this, to act justly, to love tenderly and to walk humbly with your God" (Mic. 6:8 JB).

This is the new commandment enunciated in contemporary terms: to recognize our place in the scheme of the universe, to relate to our loves with tenderness, to "do justice." Such behavior extends from a commitment to God's word, a word at work in us as a free and liberating force, discerning the thoughts and intentions of the heart, breathing new life into dry bones, piercing ruthless indifference with the good news of life in abundance.

Jesus stood up in the synagogue one sabbath and was handed this scroll of the prophet Isaiah. "The spirit of the Lord has been given to me, for he has anointed me. He has sent me to bring the good news to the poor, to proclaim liberty to captives and to the blind new sight, to set the downtrodden free, to proclaim the Lord's year of favor" (Isa. 61:1-2; Luke 4:18-19 JB). When he had finished reading, he said, "This text is being fulfilled today even as you listen" (v. 21 JB). Indeed, signs and wonders surrounded his ministry and made him a marvel to many. He gifted people with new hope and healing. His farewell gift to all of us was a share of that same Spirit that the Father would send in his name "as a guarantee" (II Cor. 5:5) that we would accomplish miracles similar to, even greater than, these. We Christians are called to continue the good news, not simply announce its promises, but make those promises real. The new earth alluded to in Isaiah and reitereated in Revelation must begin to come to pass now, for the Kingdom is established a little every day as we share with the poor, comfort the sorrowing, and introduce the "law of liberty" into societies in chains. It is a task that would terrify, if we did not have our faith, this appointment to be the continuity of a ministry well begun.

Bonhoeffer believes that the only continuity between God and his work is the Word. Creation is a product of that Word. This method of creation gives the world a susceptibility to God's word, for creation by word implies that the whole world belongs to God.[1] This is a comforting thought for believers: we are linked genetically to every other word that proceeds from the mouth of God! Formed in secret in the womb of the Word and sent forth at the pronouncement of our name, we feel an affinity for the Word that gave us life and gives life meaning. The Spirit guarantees that bond and helps us mold our behavior after the Word made flesh like us. The Word was a person like others yet different because he was wholeheartedly, in Bonhoeffer's words, a person "for others."[2] From Scripture, especially the Psalms, we glean a profile of the one who "heals the brokenhearted and binds up their wounds" (Ps. 147:3), who "will have pity on the poor and feeble, and save the lives of those in need . . . redeem their lives from exploitation" (72:13-14 JB), "who keeps faith forever, secures justice for the oppressed, gives food to the hungry, sets captives free . . . gives sight to the blind, . . . raises up those who are bowed down . . . loves the just . . . protects strangers" (146:7-9 NAB). Since all was called forth from a common source, these good deeds are already a whisper within us. "What you hear in whispers, proclaim from the housetops" (Matt. 10:27 JB). Lord, give voice to these intuitions that we may do the good that needs to be done.

There is a strong biblical tendency toward social concerns that surfaces emphatically in the ministry of Jesus and in the life of the early church. This orientation toward service rests on a commitment to a new social order at odds with the structure in power, one determined to the point of death to live by the law of love. Rabbi Abraham Heschel writes: "Frankly, I would say that God seems to be a non-religious person, because if you read the words of God in the Bible, He always mixes into politics and social issues. What is the greatest concern in the Bible? Injustice to the fellowman."[3] An issue that surfaces here involves the nature of religion. A systematic approach to God can be structured a variety of ways according to primary values. Differing perceptions are the cutting edge of a crisis of religion today. The early church was clear in its intent. "Religion that is pure and undefiled before God and the Father is this: to visit orphans and widows in their affliction, and to keep oneself unstained from the world" (James 1:27). There was always great stress on a code of behavior shaped by the gospel imperative. The twelfth chapter of Romans emphasizes genuine love, profound respect, prayer, perseverance, sharing, hard work, hospitality, humility, high ideals, blessing persecutors, treating all with equal kindness, friendship with the poor, living at peace. It may sound a bit overwhelming, but this is merely a sketch of the Christian ethic that primes us to be "for others." There is both inner change and a reaching out to change social aberrations.

It is extremely important to remember, particularly in times such as ours, that a commitment to peaceful coexistence underlies the Gospels and the life-style of those first Christian followers. The code of behavior in Romans is followed by an injunction to obey governing authorities. Of course at that time and during the years to follow, Christians lived in fear of persecution, so a low profile would have been to their advantage. Still it is significant that throughout all the early church documents, Christians are cautioned against violent resistance or aggression of any kind. They simply lived as they believed, with a quiet determination. We have moved a long way from that attitude in these angry, explosive decades, where disapproval of the power structure is tantamount to blowing it up, and the amount of blood shed for the sake of a principle seems almost irrelevant. The following passàge from a second-century document, *Letter to Diognetus,* hints at the peace and the quiet power inherent in nonviolence.

Christians are not different from the rest of men in nationality, speech, or customs; they do not live in states of their own, nor do they use a special language, nor adopt a peculiar way of life. . . . They live, each in his native land—but as though they were not really at home there. They share in all duties like citizens and suffer all hardships like strangers. Every foreign land is for them a fatherland and every fatherland a foreign land. . . . They dwell on earth, but they are citizens of heaven. They obey the laws that men make, but their lives are better than the laws. They love all men, but are persecuted by all. They are unknown, and yet they are condemned. They are put to death, yet are more alive than ever. They are paupers, but they make many rich. They lack all things, and yet in all things they abound. They are dishonored, yet glory in their dishonor. They are maligned, and yet are vindicated. They are reviled, and yet they bless. They suffer insult, yet they pay respect. They do good, yet are punished with the wicked. When they are punished, they rejoice, as though they were getting more of life.[4]

Such was the incredible contribution of Christianity to an unbelieving world! These are not phrases penned to a poster for the edification of armchair pietists but words that actually chronicle life. From pain and persecution, insecurity and insult, from the secrecy of the catacombs where no sun shines, spills forth an image of such brilliance that it dazzles the modern mind.

In a word, what the soul is to the body Christians are to the world. . . . Christians live in the world, but they are not of the world. . . . The soul is locked up in the body, yet it holds the body together. And so Christians are held in the world as in a prison, yet it is they who hold the world together. The immortal soul dwells in a mortal tabernacle. So Christians sojourn among perishable things, but their souls are set on immortality in heaven. . . . So when Christians are persecuted, their numbers daily increase. Such is the assignment to which God has called them, and they have no right to shirk it.[5]

As yeast leavens the entire loaf, so Christian communities in Diaspora spread through city after city, peacefully yet diametrically opposed to many establishment values. Their focus remained fixed on a society yet to come, and they did not seem to mind the waiting, changing what could be changed through the urgency of love, enduring without flinching that which had to be endured. Such was the stance of primitive Christianity. A voice closer to modern reality drops this equally provocative word into the heat of our revolutions. Dietrich Bonhoeffer, before his death in the prison camps of World War II, was caught up with the idea that God was teaching us to get along without God, that the God who is with us forsakes us, just as Jesus seemed to be forsaken on the cross.

147

Before God and with him we live without God. God allows himself to be edged out of the world and on to the Cross. God is weak and powerless in the world, and that is exactly the way, the only way, in which he can be with us and help us.[6]

All through the latter centuries, we Christians have turned toward a God of might, one who would redress injustice by the power of an outstretched arm and replace restrictive structures with something more suited to our advantage. We have never reconciled the dimension of suffering with personal welfare and social equity. But there are times when the notion of a suffering God conceals a wealth of meaning. There are times when our only hope is the belief that weakness conquers power, when all we can do is wait on God.

With an emphasis on deed and behavior throughout both Testaments and all through the early centuries, with such a clear call to action permeating God's spoken word, with the whole battered world crying out for help and healing, justice and liberation, why so much talk about praying? Shouldn't we perhaps call a halt to shows of piety and direct our energies toward more practical ends? Isn't it rather preposterous to think that in Belfast they set fire to candles on Sunday morning and to houses in the afternoon? Maybe we ought to forget about learning how to pray and ask the Lord to teach us how to live! Indeed it will not go well with us during those final days if our prayer is an empty facade that does not match our deeds, for God intends to examine us in love. But why separate prayer from action? Spirit and flesh are an entity. The soul is a decisive factor in how we arrange our lives. It guides, probes, sensitizes, and invariably sets the tone. Separation is a false dichotomy that must be eliminated once and for all.

Matthew Fox's provocative book *On Becoming a Musical, Mystical Bear* explores the relationship of prayer and action and makes a convincing statement for the place of prayer in our times. Since "prayer is a radical response to life," it incorporates the whole of our life's experience, our dreams as well as our deeds, what we intuit and what we attempt. Fox's reflection on the classical polarities of contemplation and action—or, as he calls them, mysticism and prophecy—is packed with contemporary insight. These opposite orientations are a constant source of tension, making demands that allow no compromise, urging us to savor a sense of presence and, at the same time, make that presence felt abroad, to be about the Father's business even as we cherish having chosen the better part. But if we remember that prayer is essentially relationship, there is no need to feel as though we were being pulled apart by both mystical and prophetic urgings. In prayer we remain rooted in the really Real even as we strive to uproot the evil we encounter all around. The friendship we enjoy feeds our enthusiasm to improve the quality of life. We face the truth that what we are determines what we do. We must be loved, be free, be healed, before we can love, liberate, heal. We bestow what we become, effectively express that which impresses itself indelibly upon us. We share what we have savored. In the transformation of the individual lies the key to transforming the world.

The time for anonymous Christianity is passing. We who care to make a difference must stand up for what we believe, boldly and unafraid, and integrate gospel values to forge a new economic order. A radical shift of priorities will precipitate a Christianity come of age in an adolescent world. A new perspective will put others first. Government policies as well as our individual life-style must be determined by a concern for the welfare of those who may live thousands of miles away. Our surplus, even our essentials, must be shared with those in need. We must beg, borrow, and deprive ourselves to honor the right of every nation to a fair share of economic exchange, allow access to resources we hoard, and not begrudge assistance to those who are given what we must earn. "In mature Christianity the grand way of contemplation will be identical with the life of action."[7] This is authentic prayer: the intelligent integration of faith and life, caring enough about the quality of life to do something about it. This presupposes a sensitivity to the content of our belief and our priorities. Such knowledge comes of reflection, when we retreat to solitude to get into touch with who we are. We cannot effectively do the Word if we do not know what the Word is asking, if we are unsure of our strengths or skeptical of our contribution. Withdrawal to reflect is not running away from responsibility, it is running intelligently to it. By drawing back, we gain perspective. In stillness we discern what is really going on. Jesus withdrew to solitude time and again to return to his task renewed. Contemplation preceded those decisive turning points of his life, and it must accompany ours.

We can make a case for personal prayer, but what about the liturgy? This is a valid question. Many voices have challenged the church on its ivory-tower attitude, assembling snug and secure in sanctuaries while the rest of the world goes by, pouring time and energy into ritual while reality is ignored, asking "Who is my neighbor?" (Luke 10:29) while day after day church-going people watch their neighbors die. It is indeed a relevant question. Tomorrow's parishioners have abandoned the church to go where the action is, telling us that while we pray for people they will get out and help them. The church has acquired the image of an exclusive spiritual club. Those who pay their dues are entitled to all the privileges of membership and little of the inconvenience. A good deal of social and psychic energy focuses inward on the group. So few people put into practice what is preached to them week after week. A sixty-six-year-old gentleman with a doctoral degree recently wrote this letter to Abigail van Buren's popular syndicated column.

Dear Abby: I am presently completing the second year of a three-year survey on the hospitality (or lack of it) in churches. To date, of the 195 churches I have visited, I was spoken to only once by someone other than an official "greeter"—and that was to ask me to please move my feet.[8]

Even though people might manipulate religion for selfish gain or gather for all the wrong reasons, this does not invalidate worship. We hold out the hope of what worship can be in order to stretch it beyond what it is. We know we cannot do God's word unless we really hear it, hear not only with our ears but with our whole heart and will. We hear best through celebration when the support of signs and symbols, the repetition of song and prayerful response, all come to focus on a single word and help to reveal its

151

meaning. In celebration, many skills and sciences are brought to bear on a given liturgical text. History, exegesis, music, art, theology, psychology, sociology, and anthropology are some of the areas involved in preparation, presentation, and response. We learn what a text meant when it was first pronounced in its historical setting. We seriously study that word. But celebration goes beyond scholarship. In juxtaposition to similar texts and through our own prayerful reflection, we encounter insights we would surely have missed had we approached the passage in isolation or less attentively. We sing, reflect, preach, and pray about the selected text of the day and in the celebrating context, struggle for a relevant application to our situation now. How could anyone participate so intensely and miss the topical point! A service of liturgy of the Word, well done, is an experience in listening, a welcome alternative to the cacophonous noise chronic to the present age. Bombarded daily with surface impressions, it is a blessing to focus our attention on just one tiny word, probing such topics as peace, freedom, love, waiting, and thousands of other possibilities for every nuance the sounds or the silence might hold. A celebration of the Word that communicates life is the best communication of the Word; it makes life a celebration.

The effort to make our worship meaningful by probing God's word for meaning will, before long, take a surprising twist and pour meaning into our lives. Hope will surface when we least expect it, disappointments will seem less ultimate. We will encounter the Word everywhere—in newspapers and poems, in editorials and books, in the theater and on the street. Once our consciousness is stimulated, we will be painfully aware that the poor are all around us. We will discover need in our own family, at the corner supermarket, surrounding us in church. If we hear the call to heal the brokenhearted, we will see critically broken people everywhere we turn, broken by tragedy or lost opportunity or crushed beneath oppressive structures that disregard basic rights. We have plugged our ears against God's word maybe because we have always known that to hear it is to be open to pain. It is hard to bear unbearable burdens, and even harder to want to help and to have to stand helplessly by. God's word is an agent of change. To hear the Word is to allow it to change us. Shaped by the Word, we will then insist on shaping life according to that Word. We become mystics and prophets, we listen and we act, and that is no easy calling. "If you make my word your home, you will indeed be my disciples, you will learn the truth and the truth will make you free" (John 8:32 JB). Celebration of liturgy or a service of worship makes us at home with the Word and exposes us to truth, broadens our arena of public prayer by sending us out into the neighborhood or in spirit to distant continents with the grace of a healing concern, stretches our sacred spaces to include all the rhythms of human life as we gather up the concerns we encounter and carry them back to church. A liturgy of the Word well done is a celebration of meaning. It is an experience in integration, revealing to us what our lives are all about. This integrating factor enables us to live rooted in reality even as we transcend it and raises our shriveled consciousness to incorporate the world.

True celebraton is never sterile, for each time we approach God's word it is never quite the same. Time has not stood still. In cyclical repetition, it sends the Word boring down deeper into the heart. When a text recurs it is different because we ourselves are different, open to shades of meaning that might have been meaningless before. The focus, the setting, the mood in which we find ourselves, have some say in the message. "I have yet many things to say to you, but you cannot bear them now" (John 16:12). Celebration helps prepare us for a revelation from the Lord. Ritual makes us ready. This is reason enough to come together. God's word is more than a memorial. It is a force, a living presence, nudging us toward communion with one another in the Lord, effecting radical conversion and a desire to redeem the world. Personal prayer strengthens us for the demands of God's word. Public prayer, celebration, helps us to hear that Word, understand its implications, and do it. How does celebration prepare us to feel and respond to need? The only way to know is through experience. Take the risk. Come and see!

Each culture has its own critical issues to consider in the light of faith. America is finally beginning to face the problem of growing old. The present crisis among the elderly is not so much a loss of youth but the fact that they are being cheated out of what was supposed to be the best years of their lives. Many scurry like hunted animals along threatening city streets, cower behind bolts and chains, spend their remaining days on earth imprisoned by their fears. Some are left abandoned to make it on their own or banished to institutions to wait in crippling loneliness until the final hour comes. "Do not reject me now I am old, nor desert me now my strength is failing" (Ps. 71:9 JB). How do we alert a youthful generation to the needs of our pioneers, create a climate that will guarantee a loving concern for all of us all our lives?

One year, toward the end of Lent, we addressed a special message to the children in our congregation. Do you love your grandmother and grandfather, we asked? Yes, they all replied. Did you know that there are grandmothers and grandfathers nearby who have nobody in the world to care about them? This was a point of some concern. Then we outlined our plan. Prepare special Easter baskets and bring them to church Easter Sunday. Each child can carry the specially prepared basket to the altar at the time of the offering and give the basket away. We need some volunteers to bring those baskets to grandmothers and grandfathers who live all alone in a big building on the other side of the city. We told the children to seriously consider whether they really wanted to do this. It would mean giving up some of their own candy and some time on Easter Sunday afternoon. They had to make a choice. They were free to say yes or no, but if they chose to participate, they had to prepare the basket themselves and sacrifice something of their own.

We repeated the rules the following week. At last it was Easter Sunday. Apparently the word had gotten around that this was a very important day. The usual crowd had tripled, so that we had to move the liturgy out of our small chapel into a big open room, where nine hundred people stood wedged together. No one seemed to mind. At the offering time, we invited all the children who had prepared baskets to come

155

forward to the altar as the folk group and the congregation sang the offering song. It was really a dumb announcement. There were no aisles, there were no spaces, just one solid mass of people. Some baskets appeared, more, many, as people in the back began passing them forward, wave after wave of baskets, large ones and little ones, boasting bright ribbons and cellophane and candy rabbits and eggs.

Then I saw a sight I shall remember all the days of my life. We had promised that the children could bring up their own baskets, so some were not letting go. When I am old and grey, I shall close my eyes and recall having said, "Only if you really *want* to share a little bit of Easter with someone who is old," and I shall picture again a sea of baskets surging forward and waves of children clutching baskets surging forward, not on the ground, but through the air, as fathers passed child after child from hand to hand up to the altar and back. A mass of movement, of color and confusion, of prayer and determination, of loving concern. "Now that I am old and grey, God, do not desert me" (Ps. 71:18 JB). The gifts were blessed, the people were blessed, the liturgy continued and was concluded, and a group gathered to deliver what turned out to be a mountain of Easter baskets filled, not only with candy, but with books and puzzles and games. The children had done a bit of research, packing their baskets with things an old person might especially enjoy. One little boy crept close to the mountain. "All that candy!" he whispered. What a way to learn that many small efforts can add up to a whole lot.

I have seen several cars full of flowers follow a hearse out of town, but that afternoon, seven cars

bulging with baskets moved in triumphant procession through the streets of Philadelphia toward the
state home for the aged. We went to the more
destitute wards. It was not a pretty sight, but the
children darted like shafts of sunshine, greeting,
smiling, coaxing a response, learning to handle
nonresponse from those too old or too full of despair.
I eavesdropped on a monologue between one little
boy and an old man closed in upon himself. "Here, I
brought you some candy!" said the child, flashing a
radiant smile. "Don't you like candy? It's good for
you. Can't you talk? It's delicious candy. I know, you
can't open it. I'll unwrap it for you. Here." Slowly,
the man took the candy. Ever so slowly, he spoke,
adding halting syllables to the child's incessant
chatter. The staff was amazed. The man had not
responded in over seven years. But on Easter Sunday
a little boy touched the little boy in him, and he was
alive again. That was some years ago, one day out of
many days, but the children still remember. All of
those who were there that day remember. We
learned a lot from that celebration, about the old,
about ourselves, about the process of death to life.
We experienced the reality of resurrection. We
helped bring back the dead. One celebration taught
us enough to change the course of our lives. Soon
after, they closed our church because of its liturgical
innovations.

It is wise to address the children. Adults learn a lot
that way. When the child is involved, the family is
involved, and everybody grows. The highlight of
Christmas for children is the presents they receive.
No amount of rationalizing will wish away the fact.
The tradition is so appealing, accept it and build on it.

Focus on the notion of gift—God's gifts to us, of life, of Jesus, our gift of ourselves to God and to each other which we express by the presents we give. Integrate this spiritual dimension with material preparations. Read, talk, sing, pray about the gift of faith, the gift of Jesus, the gift of love we give and receive every day of the year. Help the children think more of others and a little less of themselves. As they pore through catalogs preparing lists of what they hope to receive, encourage them to prepare a second list of what they plan to give, not only to friends and family, but to children they don't even know. Establish a tradition of giving to the poor in proportion to gifts received. Last year's toy is a treasure to a child who has nothing at all. Or select three toys from your enormous supply in honor of the magi's gifts to Jesus and deliver these to some agency to be distributed to those in need. Children learn by doing. We all do. "Give to others, and God will give to you. . . . The measure you use for others is the one that God will use for you" (Luke 6:38-40 TEV). Christmas is the time to "do" that Word and to work toward integration. Whenever you celebrate a particular theme, select an appropriate action that will make the Word concrete. If the focus of worship is hunger, encourage families to serve a meatless meal or a lunch of soup and bread, collect the money saved, and send it to an organization like Bread for the World. There are endless ways of sharing, of extending spiritual and material abundance to those who are deprived. If God's word is going to have relevance in these extremely skeptical times, the interpretation and application of that Word must have meaning now.

158

A minister from Chicago once told me how he had a bunch of young toughs act out the parable of the good Samaritan to help them relate to the Word. They approached the assignment with enthusiasm. They beat up the man supposedly en route from Jerusalem to Jericho. Along came the good Samaritan. The robbers returned and beat him up too. At the end of the skit, the minister asked the boys to explain that obvious deviation from the script. Their answer: "Man, when you stop to lend a helping hand in this day and age, that's the chance you take." What an insight for these times! In a sense, it was written into the parable all along. The road from Jerusalem to Jericho was a dangerous route, isolated and infested with brigands. What the Samaritan did then was no safer then the situations we face today. If our help to others involves no risk, is that especially Christian? Celebration challenges stereotype interpretation and response.

When the Lord returns at the end of time, we will be judged by the content of our actions, not by how well we said our prayers. "Come and possess the kingdom which has been prepared for you ever since the creation of the world. I was hungry and you fed me, thirsty and you gave me a drink; I was a stranger and you received me in your homes, naked and you clothed me; I was sick and you took care of me, in prison and you visited me" (Matt. 25:34-36 TEV). Do not be surprised, for "I tell you, whenever you did this for one of the least important of these brothers [and sisters] of mine, you did it for me!" (v. 40 TEV). Our place in the Kingdom will be secured by very definite deeds, deeds that flow from a life of prayer and a preoccupation with God's word. The strength of our relationship with God will be apparent from the way we live. Salvation is announced by the good works that occur in the name of the Lord. The early church attended to physical need. The contemporary church is imitating that precedent, extending the scope of its concern across continents, becoming involved in such critical issues as injustice, oppression, liberation. Responding to the word of Jesus, "I have come in order that you might have life—life in all its fullness" (John 10:10 TEV), the church is evolving a theology of liberation that recognizes, in justice, everyone's right to sustain a modicum of life. We live in a worldwide neighborhood. We are all members of the same family, children of one Father, brothers and sisters in the Lord. We are responsible for one another. This growing cross-cultural sensitivity is helping church members to think seriously about a more proportionate distribution of goods. It is no longer adequate to be charitable. Today we must learn to be just. Tossing coins to the poor means giving of our abundance. Justice means sharing whatever we have. Our dwindling supply has spawned the all too familiar complaint: "Why should I help people 'over there' when I don't have enough myself!" We have made charity an extra. When things are tight, we cannot afford extras, and charity is the first "luxury" to go. In justice, we always share a little of the little we have with those who are more in need. Christians are supposed to be recognized by their very obvious love. If good deeds are sluggish, then we might very well ask along with Paul: "Is it possible that they did not hear?" (Rom. 10:18 JB). The need is all around us and the message is brutally

160

clear. We must continually ask, What is the Lord saying, what does he ask of me?

To structure our lives by the word of God means embracing paradox, acknowledging a God whose power "is made perfect in weakness" (II Cor. 12:9), by whose bruises we are healed, in whose difficult will is our peace. The God we hail as peacemaker says: "Do not think that I have come to bring peace on earth; I have not come to bring peace, but a sword" (Matt. 10:34). The peace we were promised is not the absence of anxiety but the ability to cope with tension as we imitate the Lord who died in order to show us how to live, "making peace by the blood of his cross" (Col. 1:20). The Beatitudes turn our entire value system upside down. Everything we spend our lives working for—security, comfort, wealth—is dismissed. The situations we are told to alleviate become the conditions of grace. The poor, the deprived, the persecuted, the sorrowing—happiness is hidden here, hinting at what our attitudes should be. These be-attitudes reveal a God of paradox who speaks mysterious words, of the sinner who celebrates, the prodigal who is welcomed, the last who shall be first. If you ask this God, "Who is my neighbor?" be prepared for a surprise! Such a word needs continual probing. It is so much more than it would appear. Our own attitudes also need probing. Maybe our approach to liberation, to mention one among many concerns, needs a second look. "Liberation is the presence of a new option," suggests theologian John Yoder, "the pressure of the presence of a new alternative so valid, so coherent, that it can live without the props of power and against the stream of statesmanship. To *be* that option is to be free indeed."[9] Such a liberation presumes liberating the word of God from the shackles of stereotype interpretation and allowing it the freedom to reveal those truths contemporary to our times. "There is no chaining the word of God" (II Tim. 2:9). The Word made flesh broke all chains by conquering sin, death, the world, and freed us to follow his example. As we transform ugliness to beauty and emptiness into meaning, we ourselves will experience transformation and reflect the good we do. Chapter 58 of Isaiah should be dedicated to the doer of God's word.

> Shout to every nation!
> Proclaim integrity and liberation!
> Feed the hungry wherever they may be
> and let the oppressed go free.
>
> You shall be called rebuilder of ruins,
> make old foundations rise up strong.
> Mender of breaches, the Lord will be your song.
>
> You shall be like a well-watered garden,
> a spring whose waters won't run dry,
> giving relief to desert wastes that cry.
>
> Your light shall rise like dawn in the darkness,
> and all your shadows shall shine like noon.
> All of your wounds will feel his healing soon.
>
> Justice and peace will go then before you,
> God's glory following close behind,
> Swiftly responding, "I'm here, not hard to find."
>
> Shout to every nation!
> Proclaim integrity and liberation!
> Feed the hungry wherever they may be
> and let the oppressed go free.

Perhaps this is more than we bargained for. Such an

intense spirituality is bound to make tremendous demands, yet we dare not settle for less. As we liberate love, mend what is broken, spend ourselves in the cause of right, we do not fear the future, for we are preparing the way of the Lord.

PART TWO

INTRODUCTION

The following pages attempt a practical application of some of the many principles presented in the preceding rationale. This outline of how-to's is intended for those to whom it might be useful. It is a handbook of procedures designed to enable the inexperienced to assume active leadership in the shaping of corporate prayer. This section is meant not to be read but to be studied, digested, and applied. If you are concerned about your community worship or liturgy and determined to do something about it, trust the following process enough to risk a start. The flexibility of its structure honors traditional values as it welcomes the people's prayer.

Certain basic assumptions underlie this mini-course and form the framework for all its suggestions. These seem to me to be essential to authentic corporate prayer:

+ The validity of free expression within fixed liturgical form as perceived through traditional patterns dating back to the apostolic age.

+ The right and responsibility of all to contribute freely according to the capacity of their gift, convinced that the Spirit uses each of us for the sake of the common good, that even the unordained can and must edify and enrich the community in the context of its public prayer.

+ The contingency of revelation on insight as personal response universally applied; the eternal now of revelation on a continuum of past word and deed, present inspiration, future hope and promise. ?

+ The necessity and value of balance between innovation and continuity, improvisation and norm.

Authentic prayer is the integration of faith and action that expresses in behavior that which is impressed upon its advocates through their catalog of beliefs. Authentic prayer incarnates the sacred in very human forms and is fundamentally relationship in honesty and truth. This prayer is characterized by meaning. It defines celebration not as a "high" or "hooray" but an "aha"—daring to celebrate life and death, light and darkness, joy and sorrow, ups and downs—so that insight might make an impact on the quality of life. Whatever assists us to hear God's word can be resource for prayer together and a grace for the discerning heart. Such a prayer of the gathered community receives impetus from a style of leadership that enables shared responsibility and honors clearly delineated roles. Worship must be free, for we cannot legislate loving. If we cherish the notion of sabbath, we will want to reorder priorities and restore a right relationship, in justice, between ourselves and our world and our God.

We proceed now to prepare leaders to prepare the congregation to prepare the way of the Lord. We begin by addressing attitudes and go on to developing skills that smooth rough edges, fill in gaps, and, in general, make us ready for an unprecedented manifestation. Through a return to ancient sources and to our own resources, we worship the living God.

PREPARING THE LEADERS

Gather a core group of concerned persons from the congregation or parish. These will constitute the corporate prayer leadership team. The number is arbitrary, but be sure to keep it to a workable size. Too small can be too limiting and too demanding on time and talent. A large group is unwieldy and tends to get bogged down.

Team Membership

Criteria for choice
+ A concern for the quality of the community's prayer
+ A desire to do something to improve or sustain it

Select a representative group of about seven persons:
+ Member of the clergy
+ Person responsible for music at worship
+ Christian or Religious Education Director, if there is one
+ Young person (teen-ager or young adult)
+ Older person (senior citizen who is open to change)
+ Several enthusiastic adults

This mix ensures a broad spectrum of community representation. It includes those who have recognized roles and those who do not, touches various age levels to allow each the opportunity to contribute and be heard. Be sure to balance male and female participation and include minority representation proportionate to the larger group.

Preparation Period

Purpose

To prepare for leadership task through—
+ Instruction
  - Becoming informed
  - Growing aware
+ Skill-building
  - Discerning gifts
  - Gaining confidence
+ Team building
  - Getting better acquainted
  - Sharing insights, feelings, values

To design a program for the congregation to—
+ Improve the quality of corporate prayer
+ Enable skill-building and worship education among the membership
+ Inaugurate a process of shared responsibility for worship

A) Time frame

Agree to meet together once a week (for approximately two hours) for six consecutive weeks.

A) Program design

(Six-week preparation plan for rudimentary leadership training)

169

+ Each week, before the meeting, read a section of the opening chapters of this book (Part One). Share copies of the book, or buy one of your own. Read carefully. Make notes. Question points that are unclear or confusing or that challenge what you feel.

At the meeting

+ Discuss significant questions arising from the content read. Share feelings, fears, insights. Grapple with issues and concerns.
+ Participate in a short action/exercise that will attempt to concretize that content through practical application.
+ Close with prayer together.
+ Serve refreshments.

Process

Select a process leader who will call meetings, initiate content, facilitate the flow of events (keep track of time, see that each participant is included and is contributing).

In an effort to eliminate stereotyping, see that the process leader is other than the clergy representative who is continually cast in a leadership position. For the same reason, make sure that each participant takes a turn in providing the refreshments.

Appoint someone to take notes. Record points of special interest or concern. Save insights, ideas, and suggestions for future action.

The use of newsprint for note-taking helps the group to focus. Tape large sheets to the wall and use thick marking pens.

Content

All participants will contribute to the content

170

according to talent, training, insight, interest, experience, expertise, or just plain concern. Eventually there will be a delineation of roles. But always, there must be a climate of listening, sharing, and building on one another's contributions.

Session One
PRAYER

Prior to the meeting, read chapter 1, from the opening pages through the section subtitled "The Praying Person."

Discussion Period (approximately 1 hour)
If the size of the group is eight or less, it should be possible to have a lively discussion, all members contributing, without subdividing the group. During this initial get-acquainted stage, a single group approach is preferred for this discussion period in order to strengthen the team concept through the deepening of bonds that occurs with serious sharing.
Suggested points
(Aim for gut-level questions that get at fears and feelings.)
+ What does it mean to pray?
  What is prayer for *you?*
+ Is there really a value to silence today? If so, why?
  How would you program silence into *your* day? Be specific.
  How, where, would you structure silence into the community liturgy or service?

+ Exactly how would you aim to "pray always"?
  Give examples. Build on this as a group.
+ Allow time for individual questions and concerns.

Short Break (5-10 minutes)

Action

The following short exercises aim at getting in touch with self (which precedes our getting in touch with God and with each other).

A (10 minutes)

Take out pen and paper. Reflect on and record your response to the following questions:

+ Name an occasion that was a moment of epiphany for you (a time when God broke through and you experienced an encounter with the holy).
+ What has been consistently a source or resource of prayer for you? There may be many: a place, a person, a specific passage of scripture. Select one. Do you consciously utilize this?
+ When was the last time you really "sat still" . . . reflected quietly . . . emptied yourself . . . tried to attune yourself to the deeper you? Recently? Years ago? Ever? Be honest.
+ What do you feel is, will be, your particular gift to your worshiping community? It may be a service or a quality. Name it.

Process note

The process leader should read the questions slowly to the group, pausing after each one to allow time for private reflection and response.

172

At the end of the exercise, read the following statement to the group.

Follow-up

During the coming weeks, reflect on your responses. It has been said that we always have time for what we value. Do you personally feel shortchanged regarding your deepest values? What can you do, will you do, to restore a proper balance? After six weeks, test yourself again to determine what, if anything, has changed.

B (10 minutes)

Take time now, together, to "sit still." For ten full minutes, be silent before the Lord.

+ Get comfortable.
+ Create a supportive environment.
   Dim lights. Add a candle or two.
+ Empty yourself of all thoughts, all deliberations, as far as is possible. Just be. Wait on God. Waste precious time.

Follow-up

Resolve to spend ten minutes every day in prayerful silence. Choose an appropriate time and place. Establish a routine and stick to it. You will soon discover the difference this practice makes in your approach to life.

Closing Prayer

Invite the group to give thanks aloud. What touched you in a special way during this session? What hope do you hold for the future? Verbalize a thought or a concern or a resolution.

Invite someone to verbalize a spontaneous summary prayer.

Refreshments

Session Two

COMMUNITY

Prior to the meeting, read chapter 1, from the section subtitled "The Praying Community" to the end of the chapter.

Discussion Period (approximately 1 hour)
  Suggested points
  + Do you go to church on Sunday expecting the liturgy/mass/worship service to happen, or do you go expecting to make it happen?
    Do you feel any desire or responsibility to contribute to the corporate prayer experience? If so, is that desire being fulfilled or frustrated? Why?
  + Why is it so difficult to achieve a totally satisfying corporate prayer, one with which all the membership feels content?
    Name some disruptive factors.
    Are these present in your worshiping community?
  + Allow time for individual questions and concerns.

Short Break (5-10 minutes)

Action (approximately 45 minutes)
  The following exercise will enable the members of the group to get to know each other better. It aims at strengthening relational bonds through an honest assessment of individual orientations affirmatively done.
  Step one.
  Read aloud the section on radical/conservative,

174

Abraham/Aaron tendencies (p. 39, from "We
need more than goodwill to create community"
to p. 43, through "If our worship does not reflect
some tension, our prayer will not be real").
Step two.
Reflect individually for several minutes on the
following questions:
+ Is your own basic orientation primarily
  radical or is it more conservative?
+ Do you respond more enthusiastically to the
  unencumbered style of Abraham, or do you
  prefer a more structured way?
  Clues: How do you react to change? How do
  you handle surprises? Are you essentially inventive or do you prefer to
  follow another's lead? Are you
  enriched more by what is familiar or
  by what is new and different?
Step three.
In turn, share with the group what you feel is
your basic orientation. Give some "for instances," such as specific anticipations of,
reactions to, changing patterns of worship.

Sometimes others see us more clearly than we
see ourselves. Help each other affirmatively
sketch a personal preference profile. Since
neither tendency is better than the other but
simply reflects who we are, there is no cause to
be threatened. Value the experience and the
insights gained.
Step four.
Reflect briefly on the overall orientation of your
worshiping community. Is it primarily open to
change or hesitant to deviate from established

norms? Will the community react favorably or cautiously to your attempts at innovation?

It is essential to get at these fundamental feelings, to know exactly what the situation is in order to design a realistic worship program for the future.

Closing Prayer
Spend a few minutes in silence. Welcome spontaneous prayer.

Refreshments

Session Three
SERVICE OF THE WORD

Prior to the meeting, read chapter 2, "Living Word, Bread of Life."

Discussion Period (approximately 1 hour)
Suggested points
+ Discuss the notion of free expression and fixed form within worship.
What does this mean?
Apply the term to your own community worship.
Where is the ritual fixed or unchanging?
Where is there scope for free, personal expression?
What "gifts" might be utilized within the service/liturgy "for the common good"?

+ Discuss the statement: Religion insists on separating what God died to join.

How did Jesus use secular things as the basis for communicating his Word? Give examples.

How might we restore a truly incarnational, sacred/secular balance to our corporate prayer?

+ Allow time for individual questions and concerns.

Short Break (5-10 minutes)

Action (approximately 1 hour)

Subdivide into several smaller groups of at least three persons in each.

Invite each group to select a scripture quote from the following list, or choose their own verse, provided it is short and to the point.

+ Good Teacher, what must I do to inherit eternal life? (Mark 10:17)
+ Who is my neighbor? (Luke 10:29)
+ Lord, that I may see! (Mark 10:51)
+ Who is not with me is against me, and . . . who does not gather with me scatters. (Luke 11:23)
+ Let your light so shine . . . that they may see your good works and give glory to your Father who is in heaven. (Matt. 5:16)
+ The hour will come—in fact it is here already—when true worshipers will worship the Father in spirit and truth. (John 4:23 JB)
+ I give you a new commandment: love one another; just as I have loved you. (John 13:34 JB)

177

+ You did not choose me, no, I chose you; and I
  commissioned you to go out and bear fruit,
  fruit that will last. (John 15:16 JB)

Step one.

In separate areas of the room, small groups
should reflect together on their scripture quote.

What is this Word saying to our particular
community here and now?

How would you communicate that message?

Step two.

Design a brief prayer experience (3-5 minutes)
on your scripture's theme. Use any appropriate
resource to help the Word hit home: song,
supportive text (scriptural or other), symbolic
gesture or movement, story, verbal prayer
(spontaneous or prepared).

Step three.

Reassemble into one large group and share
prayer designs. Avoid reporting results. Rather,
let each small group lead the others in an actual
prayer experience.

Step four.

After sharing prayer designs, spend five to ten
minutes reflecting on the small group process.

Note difficulties, benefits.

What would facilitate the process for future
planning sessions?

Closing Prayer

The small group designs are the prayer for this
meeting. However, someone may wish to verbalize a summary prayer to conclude the session.

Refreshments

178

Session Four
MUSIC AS RESOURCE

Prior to the meeting, read chapter 3, "You Shall Have a Song."

Discussion Period (approximately 1 hour)
Suggested points
+ What characteristics does contemporary biblical song share with Old Testament liturgical song?
+ Discuss the current "problem" of church music.
>Is this a fair statement?
>If not, why not?
+ "Music more than any other resource makes a celebration of the liturgy an attractive, human experience."
>Discuss the validity of the worship service being attractive . . . human . . . an experience.
+ Allow time for individual questions and concerns.

Short Break (5-10 minutes)

Action
There is a definite value in the short sung refrain. Following the lead of those brief, catchy commercials whose slogans stick in the mind to surface again and again, the liturgy planner should aim to extract the thematic punch line from a biblical text and give it a musical setting. This sung refrain, repeated between the verses of an appropriate psalm, is a most effective scriptural response and

179

will linger in the memory throughout the week to recall the content of the Word.

Some background.

A musical setting should enhance the Word in worship. More important even than melody is the fundamental rhythm of the text that the rhythm of the music should support. The best musical setting is the one that makes the sung phrase sound exactly like it would if it were spoken.

Step one.

Disperse to separate rooms, if possible, as this task will be done individually.

+ Let each person recall the scriptural phrase that formed the basis of last week's small group prayer design.

+ Write a short phrase on the theme of your scripture passage, one that best captures the text's central point.

+ Repeat the phrase aloud, again and again, until you are attuned to its rhythm. Listen for stressed words and for shortened, lengthened, or accented syllables. Adjust awkward spots until your text flows smoothly.

+ Now sing the phrase aloud, just as it sounds, matching as closely as possible the textual accents to the ascending or descending line you choose. Remember, ascending notes and held notes communicate emphasis. Notes that are quickened usually do not.

Try not to be fancy or to craft a clever tune. The simpler line is usually the more effective congregational response. Just attempt to simulate the spoken phrase with your simple musical statement.

Step two.
Reassemble as a group. Share your responses. Each person in turn acts as leader of song, teaching his or her refrain to the "congregation." Repeat the refrain together several times until it is part of you. Add some spontaneous harmony, if you can.

Closing Prayer
Select one of the refrains. Sing it with enthusiasm. Spend a few moments in quiet reflection. Let spontaneous prayer arise freely out of the silence. At the conclusion, repeat the refrain again . . . and again.

Refreshments

Session Five
VISUAL DIMENSION

Prior to the meeting, read chapter 4, "Come and See!"

Discussion Period (approximately 1 hour)
  Suggested points
    + Name as many contemporary symbols as you can, both sacred and profane, and discuss their meaning.
      Do these communicate well or badly?
    + How would you go about developing a symbolic sense?
    + How would you integrate the visual dimension into your corporate prayer?
    + The Gospel of John supports those "who saw

181

and believed" as well as those "who have not
seen and yet believe."

Discuss this apparent contradiction.

What is the message here?

+ Allow time for individual questions and
concerns.

Short Break (5-10 minutes)

Action (approximately 45 minutes)

This exercise aims to encourage symbolic thinking
through the preparing of parables.

Step one.

During the first few minutes, each of you choose
an object from your purse or pocket or a nearby
table or bookcase, something close at hand,
preferably in the same room. Take the object you
select. Hold it in your hand. When everyone is
settled, proceed to the task.

Step two.

Ask yourself: What does this object remind me
of in relation to Scripture? What is it like? For
example, if you were outdoors and selected a
small branch, you might reflect: This branch is
like myself, for Jesus said, "I am the vine, you
are the branches." Or, if you selected a stone:
This stone reminds me of the one rejected by the
builders . . . or the one a loving father would not
give to a child who asks for bread.

Reflect on your object. Make a spiritual
association. Develop your thought into a short
parable or story with a particular moral for the
present. Be brief and to the point. Let the object
seen lead you to an unseen value that you will
now articulate.

Step three.
After the allotted time is up, regroup and share your parables.

Closing Prayer
In turn, verbalize a spontaneous prayer on the theme of your parable. (As "branches," you might pray for strength to endure the onslaught of the seasons, the pain of pruning; as "stones," you might ask the Lord to exchange our hearts of stone for warm, receptive hearts of flesh.)

Refreshments

Session Six
DOING THE WORD

Prior to the meeting, read chapter 5, "Doers of the Word."

Discussion Period (approximately 1 hour)
Suggested points
+ For many, the Bible is a book, and a biblical person is one who is able to quote much of its text verbatim, from memory.
   Do you agree with this?
   Discuss a more dynamic view.
+ If you were to encourage your congregation to "do" the text from Micah 6:8 as a project for the year, what practical suggestions would you make? In other words, how might your community—
   "Act justly"
   "Love tenderly"
   "Walk humbly with God"

+ How can liturgy sensitize us to local needs? How might it facilitate our involvement in social justice concerns?

+ Discuss the mystical/prophetic polarity as outlined in the chapter reading.
   Do you feel this tension yourself?

+ Discuss the Christian notion of "a new option . . . a new alternative . . . without the props of power" (Yoder) in relation to today's violent upheavals against unjust establishment values.

+ Allow time for individual questions and concerns.

Short Break (5-10 minutes)

Action (approximately 45 minutes)
   Provide a supply of recent newspapers and current newsmagazines, such as *Time* and *Newsweek*.
   Step one.
   Each of you take a paper or magazine and page through it, tearing out items that strike you as special concerns for prayer: news of violence, indifference, inhumanity, individual tragedy, environmental calamity, injustice. Select several items that touch you deeply.
   Step two.
   When the research is done, take your clippings in hand and arrange your chairs in a circle. For several minutes, reflect quietly on your areas of concern. Then proceed around the circle, placing one concern at a time before the group in prayer. Summarize your item or share its headline or, if short and especially provocative, read the entire clipping, concluding with a

phrase such as: "For this *(name it)* we now pray," to which all respond, "Lord, hear our prayer." Continue around the circle as many times as needed until all the concerns have been covered.

Step three.

Decide among you how, as a group, you might respond to these concerns with an affirmative action. Agree to assuage some hunger, alleviate a need, work to correct an injustice during the coming week. This attempt to integrate faith and life will be your prayer in action.

Note the sequence of events in this (or any) doing of the Word: awareness, prayer, action.

Closing Prayer
Integrated into the Action design.

Refreshments

PREPARING AN APPROACH TO WORSHIP

Projection

After the completion of the six sessions designed as an initial leadership training program, wait a while before meeting again in order to allow time for thoughts to settle and for some definite ideas for future directions to take shape.

Agenda for Next Meeting
Plan to meet for about three hours when you come together again. The agenda should consist of the following:

Evaluation
Examine the six-week program just com-

pleted and evaluate its strengths and weaknesses.

Synthesis of highlights emerging from the sessions
Compile a list of insights, especially pertinent
points, statements of particular meaning,
ideas to remember and develop.

Planning for the future
Set an achievable *goal* for corporate worship.
Design a *process* to achieve your goal:
Programs for instruction
Programs for skill-building aimed at shared
responsibility
Clarify *roles.*
Establish a definite *time frame* for experimen-
tation. Conclude this period of time with an
open *evaluation* and the possibility of a new
goal with different directions shaped by
community feedback.

Be sure to inform participants of this agenda well
in advance of the meeting so that all come
prepared to contribute evaluative comments and
ideas for moving ahead.

Meanwhile, those interested in further reading
material might browse in a favorite bookstore for
ideas or start by reading some of the books referred
to in Part One.

Overall Planning Session

The seventh meeting, to be attended by all who
participated in the six previous preparatory sessions, will consist of looking back and looking
ahead.

Looking Back

+ *Evaluate the six-week preparation sessions from the standpoint of both strengths and weaknesses.*
+ *List significant insights, ideas, discoveries, resulting from those sessions.*

    Try to discern and record what was really being said behind and between the lines.

+ *Share feelings, negative and positive, regarding your community worship.*

    List all the things in your present approach to worship that dissatisfy you and that you would like to change.

    List everything you find beneficial and are content to retain.

Prepare these lists together, as a team. Use newsprint for notes so that all can follow the process. Do not be inhibited or limit yourselves to what might be accepted or possible. Respond freely according to how you feel. (Be sure to keep a copy of these lists for your file.)

Looking Ahead

Study the lists of likes and dislikes, as well as the list of significant insights resulting from the preparatory sessions.

+ Through a process of evaluation and elimination, narrow down the lists to a handful of items you feel would be well worth working on. Be realistic. Do not let your initial enthusiasm tempt you to attempt too much. There will be time and opportunity to repeat this process again.

187

+ When you have reached concensus on a
  workable list of worship-related items to
  which you will address your time and
  energy, take a break.

  (During the break, have someone copy the
  list legibly, in large letters, and post it for
  all to see.)

Formulate an achievable goal.
+ After the break, spend time working on an
  achievable goal, one that is broad enough to
  encompass the items on your wish list, yet
  specific enough to be realistically possible to
  accomplish.

  Hopefully, by the time this goal is achieved,
  the congregation or parish will be ready to
  share in the process of formulating future
  goals.

Set a time limit.
+ Allow six to eight months for the accomplishment of your goal and for an evaluation
  of the process involved in working toward it.
  Even if the goal still remains to be achieved at
  the end of this specified period, meet anyway
  for evaluation and for reaffirming or restating
  the same goal, or formulating a new one.

Clarify roles and responsibilities.
+ An important part of this initial stage of
  preparation is the delineation of roles and a
  clarification of responsibilities. It is important
  that the corporate prayer leadership team
  considers itself truly a team, one that does
  indeed share a responsibility for liturgy.

Roles and Responsibilities

Factors unique to every group influence the delineation of roles. Until you determine what works best for you, try the following model and make the necessary adjustments.

Establish a liturgy or worship leadership team with rotating membership according to criteria already listed. The clergy, music, and (if applicable) Christian education representatives all have fixed membership on the team. Other team members rotate according to an agreed schedule: add one new person each month or bimonthly or after every evaluation period. Change team membership gradually, so that a balance between new members and old, inexperience and continuity, is always maintained.

+ *The minister or priest.* This person serves primarily as—

    Catalyst

    Enabling leader

    Resource and guide

      To Scripture

      To good theology

    Pastor (one who has concern) for the community

    Ultimate responsibility

      As the community's ordained or designated representative, the minister/priest is ultimately responsible for the proclamation of the Word and the celebration of Eucharist. He or she should not exercise this privilege in an authoritarian manner but as one who assists, guides,

189

and encourages the membership to contribute to the community's collective prayer.

Immediate responsibility

The sermon or homily

The overall tone of the celebration

+ *The contact person for music.* This person is the primary resource in music matters and is responsible for all music used in worship. If there is more than one person involved as choir director, organist, and leader of song, choose one to be in charge as contact person for the music team and as leadership team representative.

There are various ways to divide responsibilities among remaining team members. Two possibilities:

A. Assign a *specific area* of responsibility to each team member. For example:

Shared prayer (Prayer of the Faithful, collects, pastoral prayer, any verbalized prayer, spontaneous or prepared)

Visual dimension (ritual, gesture, movement, banners, slide presentations, etc.)

Social outreach (the link between formal prayer and action: social justice projects, etc.)

According to this pattern, team members would work separately on each service or liturgy, developing the theme within their specific area of responsibility. The task of coordinating the elements of each service would fall to the team as a whole, which would meet together, perhaps weekly, to accomplish that task.

B. Make each team member responsible for a

particular liturgy. The same person could handle the first Sunday of every month, another person the second Sunday, and so forth, or use a similar pattern of organization. For the purpose of developing this outline, we will work with model B.

As the clergy representative and the contact person for music both have ongoing, time-consuming tasks (the sermon and the music for every service), neither one should be asked to coordinate the flow of a service on a regular basis. Divide up the responsibility for individual Sundays among the remaining team members. Frequency of turn depends on the number of persons on the team.

This model allows for maximum participation and assures continuity and overall coordination. Whichever organization model you choose, remember that the role of a team member is not necessarily that of doing the task assigned but of seeing that the task gets done. As enabling leaders, team members will actively seek to include others in the planning and the carrying out of various services, perhaps arranging for smaller ad hoc committees to share responsibility for a particular Sunday.

Finally, select one person to be facilitator and contact person for the leadership team. With the exception of the priest or minister, team members should rotate through this position periodically.

Monthly Planning Session

The corporate prayer leadership team should meet monthly, preferably in the resource room (see page

242), <u>for approximately three hours, to determine
the theme of each liturgy or service for the next two
months.</u>

The first planning session will simply entail looking ahead to decide themes.

The second monthly meeting will establish the general pattern for all the planning sessions to follow.

General Pattern

+ *Evaluate the previous month's services.*

Affirm good points, successes.

Be honest about weaknesses, areas for improvement.

+ *Give a progress report.*

Examine those services already in preparation for the coming month. Let each team member present an outline of that service for which he or she is responsible in the month ahead.

Review the theme.

Make suggestions, share ideas, for music, sermon (homily) points, use of creative resources.

List the various community members who will be involved in the preparation and/or carrying out of this liturgy.

+ *Coordinate the content of these pending services.*

Check for overlap and duplication.

Ensure continuity and variety each week.

See that each liturgy is pastorally sensitive and liturgically sound.

Encourage and stimulate congregational involvement at all stages: planning, preparation, execution.

This overall coordination is the responsibility of the leadership team as a whole. Each team member should feel free to contribute suggestions and alternatives from his or her perspective.

+ *Establish themes for the upcoming month.*
The final action of the monthly planning session entails setting the themes for an additional month ahead.

Selecting a Theme

There are various ways to select a theme. Two determining factors are listed below.

+ *Free choice of text*

The prerogative of congregational churches and house churches with no fixed rite

An option for other churches on days when no specific readings are prescribed

+ *Given text(s)*

The norm for those churches with a fixed lectionary

The *choice of a text* is relatively simple. Decide upon an appropriate theme and then find supportive scriptural text(s). Since this approach means you will arrange which scripture is to be proclaimed for the common good, it is important to—

• Be sensitive to the mood and the makeup of your community
• Be alert to the liturgical and calendar seasons and to any current event that might dominate the praying community's consciousness
• Have a balanced, overall plan for the year, covering as far as possible the whole sweep of

Scripture instead of favoring unduly a particular book

Scripture is the starting point for theme selection when *a text is given*. If there is more than one text, always begin with the Gospel.

An approach

- Let one person read the text aloud to the group of worship planners. Listen carefully to the reading. Reflect quietly, and then hear the text again. Ideally, everyone should also have a copy of the text in hand.
- For the next ten minutes, brainstorm possible theme words suggested by the text. Call aloud whatever comes to mind.
- Record these words on newsprint without comment or correction.
- When you have exhausted all your ideas (for example: call, seeing, faith, take courage, and similar themes in Mark 10:46-52), review the list and select one that will serve as the focus or key for unlocking the meaning of this particular passage during this particular service, i.e., the theme to be developed in sermon, song, prayer, and other resources.
- If the lectionary indicates more than one required reading, the auxiliary texts will necessarily condition your choice of theme.

Repeat this process to select themes for services still to be planned, or design a process that suits you best.

<u>*Summary*</u>

+ *At its monthly meeting, the leadership team should exercise its responsibility for community prayer.*

194

Plan ahead two full months: Coordinate details for the first month; outline themes, exchange ideas, for the second.

Be conscious of a three-month span and look evaluatively at the preceding month; creatively at the coming month; imaginatively at the month after that.

Look occasionally at a six-month period and plan for major feasts and holidays as well as birthdays, anniversaries, and other dates significant to the community.

Name those responsible for individual services so all will know whom to contact.

+ *The monthly meeting should be an open session.*

Members of the congregation should be encouraged to contribute to the content, ensuring a rich diversity of ideas, a broader representative base, and a gradual preparation of the membership for rotation into future leadership positions.

Overall coordination remains the responsibility of the team, coordination of individual services the responsibility of individual team members who, to facilitate community involvement, might—

Work with a core committee

Approach special-interest groups (explained later on) or talented individuals for a banner or a prayer, etc.

Should a crisis situation necessitate a closed meeting, the leadership team could always arrange an executive session.

All song suggestions and music requests should be channeled to the team's music resource person well

195

in advance of the service to allow time to find the music and prepare both choir and congregation. Be flexible in your requests. It takes time to build a repertoire large enough to accommodate themed prayer.

In theme selection and planning, always emphasize meaning. Always stress prayer. Innovation is a means, not a goal. Proceed slowly at first, particularly if your parish (congregation) is conservative. Introduce variations, not just to do something different, but to assure a dynamic prayer experience. Have a good reason for every resource you use.

PREPARING THE CONGREGATION

After the leadership team has been formed, has completed the six weeks of preparatory training, and has set a goal and directions for corporate prayer, it is time to consider the congregation or parish, to decide how to deal them into the process and how to prepare them to support the change.

Approach the Community
+ *Consider the pros and cons to this timing.*
To inform the community of its goal and directions is to impose this on them and raise resentment. To incorporate a hostile community too early into the decision-making process is to risk the very real

possibility that the project will collapse before it ever gets off the ground.

+ *Decide which approach is best for your group.*

   If your congregation or parish is open and sympathetic, invite them to participate in setting a goal and directions.

      Have a good, strong process so that you reach some kind of concensus should the group be large and diverse.

      Take time. Goal formulation may require several long sessions, but it will be worth the investment.

   If a significant percentage of your community is hostile to change, suspicious of innovation, or committed to traditional forms, set up an experimental program without their active participation in planning it but well aware of and sensitive to their feelings, needs, and projected reaction.

+ *Work to offset polarization.*

   Insist that this phase is only experimental and temporary.

      There will be opportunity for all to—
         Evaluate and give feedback
         Criticize, correct, confirm

   The next step is one in which the community goes forward together or balances back.

   Insist that all give the experiment a fair trial with a degree of openness, free, as far as possible, from unreasonable prejudice.

   Insist that each opinion will be honored, will contribute significantly to the evaluation, will help to shape future patterns of prayer.

197

Whichever approach you choose, know that you risk pleasing some and alienating others. Living the gospel imperative is indeed a two-edged sword.

Introduction

Give a progress report to the community, outlining
+ What has been done
+ What is hoped can be done, and why

Instruction

Design a program of instruction that will take place prior to the first changes in your traditional worship patterns.

Possible Approaches
+ You may feel that a single introductory talk is sufficient at this time and could be handled—
  At the worship itself
  Immediately after the service
  On a designated evening
+ You may want to provide some in-depth education on the history and theology of worship from—
  The community's denominational standpoint
  A contemporary ecumenical standpoint

Suggestions
(for deepening community awareness, educating for change)
Have the leadership team summarize the training program.

Each team member take a session from the six-week program (prayer, community, etc.).

Synthesize the content under that topic into several major points.

Share the questions, concerns, hopes for the future that surfaced at the session.

Structure a period of discussion similar to the one you experienced as a team, using the points listed under those sessions. (Be sure to divide the community into smaller discussion groups.)

Arrange an open forum where the whole community might voice questions and concerns.

Set up a lecture series.

Feature outside speakers on the theology of worship, liturgy, prayer, Scripture, music, sociology of change, symbolism, etc.

Invite qualified persons within the community to share their expertise.

Preparation Period

Design a schedule that is favorable to the membership.

Arrange a series of evenings over a given period of time.

To cover designated topics

To sensitize the community to what has been projected and to prepare them for the change

Arrange an "enrichment weekend."

Cover topics in a play/pray atmosphere culminating in the Sunday liturgy (worship) where the community

Says Amen to giving the new goal and directions a try;

199

Commits itself to support community efforts tolerantly, without complaint, during the experimental period.

Enrichment

Getting better acquainted
+ *With self*
+ *With one another*

Design a program for individual and community enrichment, incorporating some or all of the following ideas.

Personal Enrichment
Take ten minutes a day, alone, for personal prayer.
　Sit in silence
　　Empty of all thoughts
　　Centered or focused on a phrase or object
　Read reflectively
　　A passage of Scripture
　　A poem or song
　　A spiritual book
　Take a quiet walk
Choose a way to become acquainted with the seasons of your heart.
Keep a journal or diary as an aid to prayer.
　Record insights, feelings.
　Copy scripture passages with special meaning, a sermon point that struck you, the verse to a favorite song.
　Write a prayer or a poem, sketch life, if you like to draw, or decorate pages with paste-ups clipped from cards and magazines.
Make a celebration booklet.
　Collect articles, clippings, paragraphs that could

For most this might be a complete new discipline!

be used in liturgy.

Arrange the booklet thematically.

List song and slide suggestions, sermon ideas, creative ways to communicate the Word.

Community Enrichment
Getting acquainted with feelings

+ *Discerning.* For a given period of time (approximately ten minutes), ask everyone to reflect quietly on the following:

  What is your single, most pressing concern regarding your community's public prayer (liturgy/mass/worship)?

  Of all the contemporary liturgical changes that you have experienced, which do you find most helpful, most spiritually satisfying?

+ *Sharing.* Form groups of four. Be sure to introduce yourselves to one another, if necessary. In turn, share your particular concern regarding worship. Listen attentively, without interruption or comment. When all have shared negative feelings, go around the group again, sharing positive feedback. (Allow thirty minutes for this exercise.)

  When time is up, reassemble as one group. Share a summary of your small group experience with the larger gathering:

  Remember who was sitting to your immediate left in your small group. It is your responsibility to report briefly on that person's main like and dislike with community liturgy (worship).

  Be very careful to share only that which is appropriate to the larger group, eliminating

201

> *strictly personal or especially sensitive comments obviously meant for the small group only.*

Ideally, capture the essence of a like or dislike in a phrase or brief sentence that can be recorded easily.

The process facilitator or group leader will record these comments on two separate sheets of newsprint for all to see: one list for likes and another for dislikes, recording each comment without identifying its source. These will be kept on file for future consideration and action.

There is a value in letting another person summarize our comments for the larger group. It demonstrates that a viable community is one whose members stand, not in isolation, but in relationship, really listening to one another, daring to support each other publicly on issues of vital concern.

+ *Closing Prayer*

Look at the phrases recorded on both lists
Reflect on them quietly for some moments
Out of the silence

give thanks for those things that have been helpful, for whatever has provided a moment of grace

ask for strength to cope creatively with the difficulties, for tolerance, patience, humor.

This spontaneous prayer should be verbalized by those in the group who feel so inclined, or summarized by the facilitator for the evening.

Skill-building

*Skill-building Suggestions to prepare for
Shared Responsibility in Liturgical (Worship) Design
and Action*
(Some how-to's in special interest areas)
Set up a series of evenings, and proceed from one
exercise to another with the same group of people.
Or schedule an occasional evening featuring a
particular topic aimed at special interest groups.

Prayers

Whether prepared beforehand or formulated
spontaneously, praying aloud within a group
takes practice. The person leading the prayer
should be mindful that he or she prays in the name
of the community and for the common good. There
is scope within some forms of verbal prayer for
very personal petitions. The Prayer of the Faithful,
or Bidding Prayers, allows for this. Otherwise the
tone and content of verbal prayer within the liturgy
should be biblically based and universally relevant.

Collects
(liturgical prayers related to the theme of the day
and directed to God for the benefit of the
community)
+ *Basic framework.* Practice writing and verba-
lizing prayers spontaneously according to
the following outline, using the given theme
as focus.
Address God (name or describe).
Give thanks and/or praise.
Recall past favor(s) or deed(s).

Ask help for present need or concern.
~~Conclude.~~

+ *Example.* Theme: LOVE

~~(Address)~~	God, our loving Father,
(Thank)	we thank you for loving us so much
	as to send us your only Son,
(Recall)	who lived among us,
	died to save us,
	and rose to assure us of everlast-
	ing life.
(Ask)	Help us to be more loving
	in thought and word and deed.
(Conclude)	We ask this in your name, God of
	love,
	through your Son and your
	Spirit. Amen.

Use this supportive framework to formulate general, unthemed prayers as well, or even the lengthy pastoral prayer that is extended simply by multiplying thanks, recollections, and needs. As you practice spontaneous prayer, keep to this basic pattern of addressing, thanking (praising), remembering, petitioning, and concluding. If you do, you will soon find it easy to write prayers or to pray aloud on the spot.

When you are comfortable with this structure, feel free to deviate from it or dispense with it entirely.

Prayer of the Faithful (Bidding Prayers)

This prayer consists of a series of petitions or invocations addressed to God for the benefit of all

PREPARING THE CONGREGATION

God's people, particularly those gathered here. The basic pattern is that of a statement by a designated leader or a petition arising spontaneously from the group, followed by a brief congregational response that is said or sung.

Pattern

It is helpful for the leader to begin with a prayer as this sets the tone and disposes the group to reflection. The leader could also verbalize the first few invocations or petitions, just to get things started.

+ *Invocations* (petitions) should move from the universal to the particular. First pray for—
  The whole world
  The universal church
  and proceed to pray for—
  A particular need
  A particular individual
  This particular community
  Remember those in the community—
  Who have recently died
  Who are presently ill
  Who are especially in need of prayer
  Remember the theme of the day, and ask that it take root in this community here and now.
+ *Response.* To each invocation, the congregation responds with a general refrain, such as: "Lord, have mercy" or "Lord, hear our prayer" or, ideally, with a phrase related to the theme of the day.
+ *Conclusion.* The leader should conclude the Prayer of the Faithful with a brief summary prayer, alluding to the many unspoken needs still hidden in our hearts.

From the very beginning, make it clear that it is not a failure if the community does not respond to an invitation to pray aloud. There should never be any pressure on the group to be spontaneous. Some people—and from time to time, all people—prefer to pray in silence, and we must learn to be comfortable with that.

Suggestion

Those who desire to develop the skill of writing prayers or praying spontaneously in a group should elect to come together several times to practice the above exercises. Practice praying aloud over and over until you become accustomed to hearing the sound of your voice in the context of corporate prayer. The results will be well worth the effort.

Themes

We need to sensitize ourselves to the notion of theme. The community will need special help in learning to filter out good but extraneous content in order to focus narrowly but deeply, again and again, on just one of God's words.

Theme Selection

Encourage members of the parish or congregation to come together for an evening of skill-building in selecting themes.

+ Brainstorm a given text for all possible theme words apparent to the group (process described under "Monthly Planning Session," page 195).

Read the text aloud.

Reflect quietly.

Share aloud—and record—themes suggested by the text.

Use a text with a lot of imagery during this practice session so that people can discover for themselves the many ways there are of approaching a single text. (Try Isa. 9:5-7; Mark 10:42-56; John 14:1-7; 20:19-29)

+ When ideas have been exhausted, do not narrow down the suggestions to a single theme, but post the entire list for all to see and move on to the next exercise: Theme Development.

Theme Development

+ Divide the assembly into smaller groups of three persons (or more, if the total group is especially large).
+ Small groups: study the list of theme words, and select one that strikes you. You will work with that theme for the rest of the evening.
+ When the groups have all chosen a theme, let a representative from each group come forward to circle and initial that word. Once a theme is taken, make an effort to avoid duplication by choosing from among the others on the list. However, do not be concerned should several groups prefer the same theme as it will be interesting to see how each one develops.

A. Tracing a Theme Through Scripture (approximately 45 minutes)

With just a little practice, you will soon be adept at finding your way thematically through Scripture.

Materials needed

Bibles—enough for at least one per group
Concordance—a complete edition and several abridged editions for group use
Paper and pens

Before beginning

Familiarize yourselves with the use of a concordance. Once mastered, it will save you precious hours locating that favorite but elusive scripture text. Remember, each concordance is designed for use with a specific translation of Scripture. To find a passage, make sure the concordance you are using matches the Bible translation you have in hand: Revised Standard Version, Jerusalem Bible, etc. Once you have located your text, you can refer to one or several other translations for the most effective rendition.

Task

Gather in small groups, with Bible and concordance, in separate areas of the room.

Search for five additional texts (not the one from which your word was originally chosen) relating to your theme. Be selective. Make sure your choices say what you want to say. Use a variety of biblical books.

Edit the texts you select to approximately three pertinent sentences each.

Write a short, punch-line phrase that captures your theme and links all the passages you have selected.

When your task is complete, reassemble into one large gathering and share results in the following manner: a representative of each small group in turn will teach the short, spoken response, or

PREPARING THE CONGREGATION

punch-line phrase, to the large group and will then read the theme-related texts, following each text with that congregational response. Note the richness now added to he original scripture text

+ Through the variety of themes
+ Through the depth of each theme's development

(If time and energy permit, take a break and then go on to the final exercise. Otherwise, plan to meet again another time.)

B. *Designing a Worship Module on a Theme* (Structured) (approximately 1 hour)

This exercise has already been described under "Preparing the Leaders," session three (page 179), but because of several modifications, it is repeated here.

+ In separate areas of the room, each small group should reflect together on the theme word previously chosen and developed in the preceding exercise. Try to answer these questions in concrete terms:
  • What is this Word saying to this particular community here and now?
  • How would you communicate that message to the community so that it might be truly heard and acted upon?
+ Spend sufficient time on the basic question before moving on to the more practical how-to's.
  • Design a brief prayer experience (3-5 minutes) on your theme.
  • Use the original scriptural text.
  • Enlarge one of the auxiliary texts already

chosen, and use your scripture-verses-with-refrain module as a response to the reading.

- Use any appropriate resource that will help the Word hit home: song, symbolic movement, story, spontaneous prayer, etc.
- Set your short refrain to music. (See "Preparing the Leaders," session four [page 180] for a descriptive how-to.)

+ Use several or all of the above suggestions in your prayer design and incorporate ideas of your own.

Reassemble into one large group and share your designs. Take turns leading the "congregation" in prayer, according to each group's developed theme.

After all the prayer designs have been shared, spend a short time reflecting together on the small group process. Note particular difficulties as well as those things supportive to the accomplishment of your task.

The above approach to theme development and liturgy design is fairly structured. It is meant to be so. The aim here is not so much that of creativity but of mastering the basics. Too little time and attention has been spent in training the average parish or congregation to be comfortably involved in the fundamentals of prayer together and in encouraging all to contribute according to each one's capacity under the guidance of the Spirit. Too much stress has been and continues to be placed on the new, the innovative, the different, with the result that shared responsibility for the preparation and actualization of corporate prayer is still a long way from taking root in the majority of our parishes and congregations.

What is new about contemporary worship is the discovery that it is *ours,* that it must *mean* something to *me* if I am to be enticed to embrace its demands and live them, and that this "me" within the context of corporate prayer is always conditioned by the qualifier "we," with all that this implies.

Practice the preceding exercise more than once, until you are at ease with its expectations. Then move on to the following which will stretch your creativity just a little bit more.

Designing a Worship Module on a Theme (Unstructured)
This exercise is similar to the one above, but its approach is a bit freer, and it aims to stimulate you to think creatively.

+ Begin with a list of *WORD-verbs,* verbs that are selected at random from Scripture and contain in their one-word simplicity the essence of the biblical message. Find your own, or use the list below for a few of the many possibilities.

strengthen	love	give	redeem
visit	reach out	thank	remember
call	forgive	ask	praise
touch	build	proclaim	provide
heal	send	obey	care
inspire	suffer	follow	seek

+ Form into smaller groups of three persons (or more, if the total group is especially large).
+ Select a WORD-verb that especially interests

211

your group, one verb per group. Do not let
the other groups know your choice.

+ Give the verb a scriptural context, that is,
find a biblical text in which this verb is
central, one that provides the verb with a
particular nuance. This will be the message
that your group must communicate. Keep it
short! Write the text down.

+ Be careful to keep its contents concealed from
those outside the group.

+ Small groups move into separate rooms to
design a brief, three-minute, *nonverbal* prayer
that will communicate to others the essence
of your scripture text. Involve everyone in
your group, and make an effort to incorporate the larger group into the final action.

An Example
The WORD-verb. "Send"
The scripture.
"The Spirit of the Lord God is upon me, [and]
has sent me to bind up the brokenhearted, to
proclaim liberty to the captives" (Isa. 61:1).
The action.
One group approached the text this way. All
knelt in the center of the room. Then one person
stood up, took a cigarette lighter from his
pocket, lit it, then raised and lowered it over the
head of each member of the group in the manner
of descending tongues of flame. The small group
arose, moved out among the larger group, raised
several people to their feet, laid hands on others,
blessed still others. And that was all.
Asked to select the corresponding text from a

list of choices, all guessed correctly. The symbolic action used here communicated the essential message though not a word was spoken.

+ When preparation time is up, reassemble into one large group and hand your scripture texts, still concealed, to the facilitator, who will copy all the texts onto newsprint. If the facilitator does not participate in the actual task, he or she could copy these texts when the small groups are otherwise involved and save a bit of time. The facilitator should also add three extra texts to the list, so that if there are seven groups, ten texts should be posted.

+ Each group in turn should make its presentation to the assembly. At the close of each action, try to guess the correct scripture reference. You must come to a concensus. Only one choice per presentation. Continue the process until all the presentations and guesses are completed.

+ Check the results. How accurate were your guesses? How effective were the small group designs? Evaluate the presentations.
   Name those actions especially effective.
   Suggest alternatives for anything that was unclear.

+ You have just completed a practice session in symbolic thinking, a relief perhaps to those tired of too many words. You are ready to move from the verbal to the visual dimension.

Visuals

Symbols, ritual gesture, photography, art: all are

213

essentially visual, leaning on sight not speech to foster insight. What follows are a few suggestions on how to sharpen visual sensitivity through the wonderful world of images, in order that we might better perceive what God envisions for us.

The Camera

Whether your camera is a simple Instamatic or a single lens reflex, pocket-sized or equipped with the latest accessories, you too can catch life off guard and single out its most precious moments for reflection and celebration. A camera's contribution is its unique ability to coax us to look very close, to center in, edit out, focus on life in small bits and pieces: a smile, eyes, a single flower. Probe what these have to say to us about ourselves, each other, God.

Field Trip: A Camera Walk (approximately 2 hours)
On a clear Saturday or Sunday afternoon, any season, meet at a central location. Load your camera with a roll of outdoor slide film.
Plan a walking trip outdoors in a park or wooded area, although there is much to be seen and contemplated downtown or in your own neighborhood, even in your own home.
Your goal is to chronicle a sliver of life as it presents itself to you on this particular day. Think small. Think close. Think characteristic. Be a poet in pictures.
    If you want to capture a tree, focus on a branch or its bark.

214

If you want to record loneliness, look for dry, trampled leaves; an isolated lamppost; an unoccupied bench; or someone walking, small and unaccompanied, across a vast, unyielding landscape.

Shoot scenes as they strike your fancy, or proceed with a very definite idea in mind, perhaps a text you intend to illustrate, in which case the stroll becomes a hunt to find the perfect image.

Sharing the Results

When your films are developed, schedule an evening for sharing the results. Project the slides on a large screen for maximum clarity and for an experience of being absorbed into the picture and its environment.

Note instances where the camera failed to see what you saw.

On the other hand, notice the many surprises—details you had missed with your impatient, superficial eye.

During refreshments, brainstorm possible uses for your slides. Decide on a future project and plan to meet again.

Picturing the Word

Tapping the visual sense is a good way to link the sacred and the secular, to integrate faith and life through concrete expressions that particularize the Scripture's perennial norms in our down-to-earth here and now.

Illustrate a text:

Prepare a text on a particular theme. Write your own, or juxtapose bits of scripture with passages of a poem or other provocative reading. Add a sung refrain or tape some suitable background music to play softly as the text is being read. Some very visual themes include:

Creation   Old age
Seasons   Need versus plenty
Faces   Water: its many moods
Children

Communicate meaning through slides that either concur or contrast with the text. Do not be easily satisfied.

The slide you finally select should feel exactly right. A picture of poverty will convey a situation of need, but a visual of sheer opulence against a text that tells how millions starve will really have an impact. Sometimes the best way to communicate freedom is to show a person in chains.

Illustrate a song:

+ Listen to the song "If You Look" on the album *Seasons* by the Medical Mission Sisters.

 The song is an invitation to look deep into the ordinary, to penetrate surface impressions, to go to the core of every experience in our insatiable search for meaning.

 What does the song say to *you*? What illustrations would you add to release its meaning?

+ Select those slides that you feel really fit the text. This may take some time. You might have to search, borrow, go out again, and shoot another roll of film. Keep at it until you are absolutely satisfied. When you are, try it out on friends. If they agree, your task is done. You have achieved the difficult balance of articulating a personal response that is universally relevant.

+ Integrate your visual presentation into a community prayer experience. Play the song on your stereo. Better yet, convince a small group to learn the song and sing it live. Welcome feedback at the end of the session.

There are as many pictorial versions of a text as there are individuals, for it is all a matter of perception. Our way of seeing reflects who we are and the way we interpret life. Slide presentations then are very personal meditations that we elect to share. The important thing is that each approach be appropriate to the message discerned and true to the vision seen.

There are many songs suitable for slide illustration. Once you begin to listen and look, you will quickly make connections you had missed before. Meanwhile, as that sense is sharpening, try illustrating the following parable.

+ Listen to the song "Who Is My Neighbor?" also on the album *Seasons.*

The verses tell the story of the good Samaritan as related in Scripture.

Why not introduce your own cast of characters and present them through the camera's eye?

The refrain repeats the question that necessitated this parable as response: "Who is my neighbor?"

What would be your visual reply to this insistent inquiry?

+ Again, firm up your presentation, get a

group to learn the song, and take your prayer module to the community.

There are many ways to tell the good Samaritan story, which is as pertinent today as it was in biblical times. My own pictorial version is a rerun of the original that returns to the old Jerusalem-Jericho road and casts local people in the decisive roles and various cultures in the recurring refrain. It could have been filmed as effectively on Broad Street in Philadelphia or on any of the many streets on which we continue to pass need by. The camera is a liturgical attempt to link faith to action. Lord, that we may see!

Mechanics:

In all fairness, I must add a note of mechanical warning and some practical do's and don'ts.

+ Do be prepared for disaster to happen. When you are prepared, it seldom does.

Bring a spare projection lamp in case the light blows.

Carry an extension cord with you so that you can reach the plug which is almost always on the opposite side of the room.

Bring masking tape to tack down loose wires, or people are bound to trip.

Be sure the lid on your carousel tray is tight so when it tips over the slides won't spill.

Don't forget that flashlight if you want to read the script when all the lights go out.

+ Don't let machinery upstage your presentation. As far as possible, keep your projector inobtrusive, preferably out of sight. Avoid a theater atmosphere. Church people resent

opening the sanctuary to whatever is secu-
larly successful and to anything that smacks
of gimmick.

+ Do aim for the largest, clearest picture
possible.
Make sure the room is dark.
Use a white wall, instead of a screen,
whenever you have a choice. This allows the
images to emerge during prayer as if from the
imagination with no apparent technological
assist. If you must use a screen, try to find a
large one. Miniature visuals are seldom
prayerful. Position the screen where it will
be least offensive and visible to all.

+ Remember to focus the image! Our ideas
might be blurry, but that should never affect
the slides.

Throw a Picture Party

This is best done at the close of summer when
people are eager to reminisce about past trips and
vacations. A great way to share worlds and to build
up your community's slide library! It can deepen
the bonds within community as we take the less
traveled among us to places they have never been.

Invite the congregation (parish) to a do-it-your-
self slide-showing evening.

Limit the time and/or slides per person (ten or
twenty minutes is best), depending on how
many persons show up to show and tell.

Encourage people to bring significant slides,
ones that tell the story. Avoid excessive coverage
of the family pet or Aunt Mabel, and do leave
those fuzzy ones at home.

Make a note of the best of each set shown. Ask the

photographers if they would be willing to donate duplicates to the church's slide library. (Usually, people are delighted to do so.) Photo credit would be given each time the slide was used.

This is a quick, inexpensive way to build up a community slide collection on various subjects and themes. It is also a way of sharing talents that ordinarily are confined to small slide boxes on dusty shelves. You might alert particularly good photographers to subjects of special interest. Many are only too glad to have a photographic assignment in order to indulge their hobby.

A Festival of Films

There are many good, provocative short films available free through your library service or through rental from various publishing houses. *The Dancing Prophet, The Red Balloon,* and *The Stringbean* are great catalysts for discussion, provide a forum for symbolic exploration, and offer an excellent medium for communicating the Word.

Show one film a week for four weeks outside of the structured liturgy, unless your community is already prepared to consider the experience prayer.

Follow the film with a discussion period. Probe the various scenes and suggestions. Challenge appearances. What did they really mean?

Determine how and when you might incorporate a film into your service of the Word.

Schedule a day-long marathon. Show half a dozen films. Saturate your senses with new levels of meaning. Does the Word ever touch you as strongly or as deeply as a well-made film?

Banners

This is too extensive a topic to be treated here. We introduce this valuable visual aid in passing. It is up to you to follow through on it.

Arrange for a banner-making party.

Form a banner-making club among the artists and seamstresses of the community.

Invite a local artist to give some guidance in the art of making banners.

Read some of the many books available on the subject.

Add a touch of color and playfulness to your place of prayer. Dare to overwhelm the eye with meaning. This sense still has a lot of influence on the heart.

Music

Ideas for skill-building and community enrichment in the area of liturgical music.

Repertoire

There are many ways to build up a viable repertoire. Research, rehearsal—it all adds up to work and determination, but it can also be a lot of fun. Try some of the following suggestions for increasing your congregation's musical capacity.

Sponsor an occasional song fest, preferably outdoors around a campfire when weather permits.

+ Sing old favorites, any category.
+ Learn some Bible songs that can later be used in church.

+ Encourage local talent—
To bring instruments
To participate in a brief talent show
To teach and lead the community in a favorite song

The accent here is on fun, singing for the sheer joy of singing, with no other practical purpose in mind, except perhaps the rediscovery of a simplicity we had lost. Many of us have forgotten the warm bonds forged by sharing a common song.

Have a monthly hymn-sing (folk-style songs included) in a more formal setting with some definite goals in mind.

+ Plan to learn the new material needed for the coming month's services.
+ Make sure the choir and/or core group is well prepared in advance.

Even if the attendance is not enormous, those who do come will help carry the sound of new and unfamiliar material in the weeks ahead. Serve refreshments. Church music can be fun!

Organize an ad hoc group of persons interested in searching for new and suitable songs.

+ Plan to spend a day browsing in your favorite music store.
+ Peruse all the new music available, dividing the task among you.
+ Study the text first. Only if the words are acceptable—liturgically appropriate, relevant, inspired—will the song be considered a possibility.
  Criteria for choice:
  Suitable text

Singable music
Right for your congregation
+ Arrange to stop for lunch. At that time, discuss the possibilities and narrow the field before returning to the store to—
Review
Evaluate
Eliminate
Purchase within the limits of what your budget can afford

Sponsor a scavenger hunt. Invite the whole community to participate.

+ Issue a list of ten themes (love, peace, forgiveness, etc.).
+ Award a prize to the first person who returns the list completely filled in with a song suggestion for each of the themes. To win, the songs must—
Be new to the congregation (not part of the present repertoire)
Meet established criteria
Good text
Good tune
Good theology
Good for this congregation

Let the leadership team act as panel of judges. Repeat the scavenger hunt again later on. Simply prepare a list of new themes or repeat several of the more popular ones that welcome variety. Sponsor some seasonal searching: songs for Lent, Easter, Christmas. The community will be less hesitant to learn new material if they have been involved in its selection.

Write your own songs.

This entire process looks interesting & workable

if the congo seeks to elevate all of its energies in this area!

This is a good way to build up your repertoire. Try these ideas:

+ *Schedule an antiphon or refrain writing session* to encourage the weekly setting of a short, easy-to-learn, thematic, congregational response. (See pages 181-82 for a description of the process.)

Invite people to bring to the session a favorite scripture verse. It is more exciting to practice on a phrase that is really meaningful to you.

Sponsor a song-writing contest. Have several categories:

+ Original text and melody by the same person
+ Original text and melody in collaboration (lyricist and composer)
+ Original text, melody in public domain (that is, a melody old enough to have outlived the terms of copyright and now available for general use)

Schedule an evening when the finalists in each category present their songs before an audience. Select the winners. Award prizes. Use the winning entries in future liturgies.

Arrange a day-long song-writing workshop if local talent and interest warrants it. Collaborate with neighboring churches. Invite outside expertise.

Evaluation

Organize a task force to evaluate the community's present music repertoire, particularly from the standpoint of text.

+ Is the theology acceptable?
+ Is the language relevant, archaic, out-of-date?
+ Can you identify with this text now, or is it

224

simply a nostalgic flashback to the past? A good test is to ask yourself: Do I really believe this? Would I recite this text—recite it, not sing it—as my own personal theology, publicly, among my peers? Give marks to indicate high and low priority songs. If your congregation uses a standard hymnal, be prepared for some surprises! Be brutally honest, even if it means you may have to relinquish some of your favorite hymns.

Update best-loved, traditional hymns whose questionable theology might preclude continued use.

+ Check the date of composition. Chances are it is a traditional tune already in public domain and you will be free to work with it.
+ Ask your local poet to retouch the text or write a new one.

Contributions

Prepare a shelf list of all the hymns and songs sung by the choir as well as those which are known by the congregation.

+ Categorize them according to theme.
+ Cross-reference each piece under all pertinent classifications.

This will be a valuable reference for all liturgy planners. File it in the resource room.

Encourage people to give a gift of music to the community.

Caught in the copyright impasse? Afraid you won't be able to afford the songs you want to buy? Here is one solution.

+ Encourage community members to "buy" a song and give it to the church, much as you might donate flowers or invest in a living memorial such as a window or a pew.

+ Most publishers charge a minimal fee for permission to reprint a song or else supply ready-made word sheets at a cost below that of local duplicating and well within the budget of most people, including the very young.

+ Appoint someone to handle the secretarial work. He or she would maintain a current address list of various publishers, as well as a file on how and where permissions for use might be obtained.

+ Make mention of the donor on the day the new song is introduced. For example, your bulletin or calendar might read: "Today we will sing 'Let There Be Peace,' gift of Ann Olsen. Thank you!"

+ This community-building idea will—
  • Develop a sense of responsibility and personal commitment among the membership with regard to the songs you sing
  • Encourage personal initiative and reward it with public affirmation
  • Stretch your community music budget so that the burden of expense is shared
  • Assure musical variety through a wide representation of tastes

Be sure to set some limitations. A song cannot become part of the community's permanent repertoire unless, in the judgement of a representative group, it meets basic criteria. If the song merits a place in corporate prayer, the

226

individual is given the go-ahead to purchase it and gift it to the church.

Give a gift that keeps on giving, one that lives on and on!

Leadership

The musical quality of a group depends to a large extent on its leadership.

Music team

+ Choir director
+ Organist
+ Leader of congregational song
+ Guitarist(s)

Some of these roles can be combined provided responsibilities do not overlap and require simultaneous execution. If you do not have a competent guitarist in your congregation or parish, hire one.

Choir

More than ever, contemporary worship needs a dedicated choir

+ To lead and support the community in congregational song
+ To assist the community in the ongoing task of learning new music
+ To enrich the standard repertoire by adding new harmonies to familiar pieces on special days
+ To edify and inspire through a musical presentation well done and, therefore, to enable prayer (by means of a reflection song after Communion, during the liturgy of the Word, as a prelude to the service and related to the theme of the day)

With the heavy repertoire demands of today's themed liturgy, the choir can alleviate some of the congregational burden by singing the verses of those songs that are structured according to verse and refrain. In turn, choir members can enrich the congregational refrain with harmonization.

It is important to avoid any connotation of performance or entertainment. The choir does not perform. It uplifts. It is equally important to correct false notions of participation. To participate fully does not always mean being active. Sometimes just to be still is more than enough. Inner activity is seldom apparent. At a symphony, I participate in the experience as deeply as the cellist although I never play a note. Now that we have reclaimed our rightful active role, let us not exhaust ourselves by overdoing to the opposite extreme. Choirs, we still need you to help us listen and learn. Do continue to preserve and present to us the musical riches of our past.

Core group

In addition to the choir, a community is well served by a smaller, more flexible core group dedicated to contemporary styles and sounds. Their enthusiasm can often move the most sluggish congregation to some initiatives. The core group should—

+ Have a position of visibility
+ Have sufficient amplification to be understood but not enough to distract or disturb

The core group, guitarists, and leader of song are all closely related, as are the choir director and the organist. Good teamwork that results in a unified approach will do much to foster musical cohesiveness among choir, core group, and congregation and will make a difference in the sound of the singing.

The core group with its leader of congregational song alternates musical leadership in the service with the choir and its director. Ultimately, however, all are part of a single team whose primary aim is to enable the community to pray through music.

Forum

The following is an attempt to respond briefly to some perennial concerns about music. These seem to surface in the form of questions over and over again. There are no satisfactory answers, merely hints at means and directions toward solutions you yourselves must find.

How can we get our congregation or parish to sing?
For starters:

+ Motivate people to want to sing by providing them with some enjoyable experiences of community singing, preferably outside of church—

    Song fests

    Song learning parties

    A candlelight carol-sing at Christmas

+ Prepare people through your religious education program to accept and welcome song as a way of life. Use song to teach the parables and to integrate biblical texts with daily demands.

+ Introduce your community to good songs right from the start. Encourage feedback and

229

song suggestions. Try some of the skill-building ideas presented earlier on.

+ Employ good teaching techniques.
+ Include enough variety to avoid monotony but not more than the community can handle.
+ Try some learn-in-an-instant songs in which the participation of everyone is essential and yields a rich, harmonic sound.

See "Song of Praise" (reprinted in Appendix). You will find that even a nonsinging parish can handle this with ease.

+ Insist that people memorize words. Sing without books or papers right from the beginning and patiently suffer those initial mistakes.

A song once committed to memory is never really forgotten.

A song learned by rote tends to return throughout the day at the most unexpected times and places to help us integrate our prayer and our workaday world.

Rote learning requires effort. But until we commit a song to memory, it is never really ours, although we might sing it year after year. Test yourself. How many of your favorite hymns can you sing from memory beyond the first or second verse? The songs we carry within us are the very songs we sing on all the many occasions when we do not have our books. We like to sing the songs we know. We know those songs we like to sing.

PREPARING THE CONGREGATION

+ See that the core group and choir truly support but do not dominate congregational singing.

> Convince the community that you really need them. Prove it by stepping back from the microphone during the congregation's part.
>
> A community that is too dependent on the leadership's sound will eventually stop singing.
>
> Have the choir occasionally infiltrate the community to assist the singing right there in its midst. It is hard not to sing when the star alto is bellowing in your pew.

+ Encourage a reluctant congregation to sing by positioning a song leader right in front of them, one who insists on a response through—

> Eye contact
>
> Conducting
>
> Sheer personal dynamism
>
> A sense of presence and a confidence that communicates that this song will indeed work and that it is going to be good
>
> The leader of congregational song has got to be clearly visible and impossible to ignore, comfortable in front of people, convinced that the community can and will sing well.

How can we get our congregation to sing contemporary music? It resents the folk-style form and forbids the use of guitar in church.

+ Begin by helping the congregation understand both the folk form and the guitar.

Put them in a historical perspective.
Defend their age and their continuity right down to the present time, but do not be defensive.
Remind people that David and the psalmists prayed with strings and in a decidedly human style; that Martin Luther's favorite instrument was the stringed lute.

+ Avoid a hard-sell attitude. Insist there is no one kind of music right for prayer. The concrete expressions of a form make it good or bad. No style should be automatically canonized or, on the other hand, dismissed. Every form deserves a chance, even the so-called folk style. Suggest a trial period. Agree to abide by the community's evaluation after giving the contemporary style a full, fair chance. After all, music is a prayer response of the people, and it would make little sense to impose on people a form they do not really want, provided they know it well enough to know they do not want it. Be open with your community. Acknowledge their feelings and sympathize with their fears as you try to lead them gently forward for their own personal and spiritual good. Your goal is at the very least a climate of tolerance. As a community committed to gospel values, you could hardly settle for less.

+ Introduce the skeptical congregation to contemporary music gently, by means of so-called bridge songs that overlap both traditional and contemporary sound and are acceptable to both.

232

"Take This Bread" (see Appendix)
"God Gives His People Strength" from the album *Joy Is Like the Rain* by the Medical Mission Sisters
"Children of the Lord" from the album *In Love,* also by the Medical Mission Sisters (see Appendix)
These songs can be sung with the organ until the community is ready to attempt the transition to guitar.

How can we have continuity in a transitional community always in flux?

This is a tough situation, characteristic of college and university communities that feature a high degree of mobility. Nevertheless, a balancing factor in these same communities is the deep level of commitment and enthusiastic support that many other churches lack. Some of the structural suggestions already made provide both continuity and flexibility and would be particularly helpful here.

+ The leadership team allows for stability and movement.
+ The concept of shared responsibility by means of enabling leadership calls for continual talent turnover and is designed to deal with change.

You may have to keep reteaching the same songs, but the above structures at least assure that singing will survive.

What about the use of secular songs in worship (liturgy)?

Again, be careful of those categories. To label a song "secular" is as tricky as calling another one

233

"sacred." The factors that shift a song toward either pole are seldom clear-cut.

+ In general:
    If a song fits liturgically,
    If it unlocks meaning,
    If it uplifts, inspires, and helps to integrate,
    Use it!

+ The notion of theme is an aid here. It helps to erase arbitrary boundaries separating what is and is not suitable. A theme approach validates an otherwise inappropriate choice. The key word again is "meaning." The aim is integration. So-called secular songs must lift up and touch transcendence. Traditionally sacred songs must stoop down to inform the horizontal in a truly incarnational sense. But then we would no longer have that sacred/secular distinction, would we?

Summary

We have said a lot about music as resource and have left so much more unsaid. The turbulent drive that brought us to our current theology of worship has taught us a lot about our song.

+ We know now that our cautious, negative tendencies within worship stem from a continuous historic struggle, that our rules were written by human hands and are not tenets ordained by God.

+ We are discovering that liturgical change is not the end of the struggle but in fact the beginning, heralding an ongoing search for meaning that must constantly strive to

balance the traditional and the new.
+ In our liturgical music, we must continually guard against—
  • The boredom of routine patterns—
    The singing of the same of songs
    That four-song syndrome that stalks the Mass, stifling dynamism as effectively as any previous mold.
  • The sterility of the "correct" hymn that plays it safe "up there" amid angels and clouds in the starry skies far from the failing, sweating struggle of the human condition
  • The inflexibility of precise wording that plays around with syllables, stressing exactitude to such an extent that we no longer remember what we were going to say

There is comfort in knowing that the problems we encounter have surfaced many times before. In the preface to *Sacred Melody,* Charles Wesley offered these tips for congregational singing back in 1761:

"Sing lustily and with good courage. Beware of singing as if you were half dead, or half asleep; but lift up your voice with strength. Be no more afraid of your voice now, nor more ashamed of its being heard than when you sung the songs of Satan . . . and take care not to sing *too slow.*"

Social Outreach

The practical application of all our efforts to be a truly praying community, the consequence of a deeply rooted liturgical spirit, is the visible integration of behavior and belief.

235

Each community must answer for itself:
What are the needs to which we must respond, both locally and abroad?
Who are the hungry and what will we do about it?
Who are the victims of unjust, oppressive structures and what plans have we for liberation?
Who are the critically broken? How can we help or heal?

Structure awareness sessions
Where the uninformed can learn about the exploited, the abused, the victims of discrimination.
+ Gather reports and statistics.
+ Subscribe to publications that will keep you informed.
+ Keep a bulletin board up-to-date with the most pressing social concerns.

Design a program of social action
that will reach out into the neighborhood and benefit those abroad. Motivate one another to get involved.

Suggestions

Here are some additional aids to improving the quality of your public prayer.

Proclamation of the Word
Try having a separate service of the Word each month for children, youth, and adults.
+ All meet together in church as a community for the opening ritual of your customary Sunday service.

+ Proceed to separate rooms for the proclamation of the Word.

>Use the same text and theme for all.
>
>Be sure you have a real service of the Word, not a classroom exercise.
>
>*Each group should have a minister of the Word.*
>
>*Qualified laity can fulfill this role.*
>
>Encourage participation in the homily or sermon through dialogue, shared reflection, role playing, or song.

+ Regroup in church as a community at the offertory, or at the Holy, Holy, or just prior to the Communion rite if Eucharist is to follow, or simply regather for the final prayer, benediction, and song.

Try proclaiming the gospel in song.

Use a small group or the entire congregation or both in the event of verse and refrain. The parables are particularly suited to a sung presentation, as so many narrative ballads attest.

Here are some gospel texts set to music. From time to time, design them into your corporate prayer.

+ *Parable of the good Samaritan* (Luke 10:29-37)—"Who Is My Neighbor?" (from the album *Seasons*)

+ *Parable of the prodigal son* (Luke 15:11-32)—"Ballad of the Prodigal Son" (from the album *I Know the Secret*)

+ *Prologue to the Gospel of John* (John 1:1-14)—"In the Beginning" (from the album *Gold, Incense and Myrrh*)

+ *The Beatitudes from the Sermon on the Mount*

237

(Matt. 5:3-12)—"The Beatitudes" (from the album *In Love*)

+ *Parable of the Wedding Banquet* (Luke 14:15-24)—"The Wedding Banquet" (from the album *Joy Is Like the Rain*)

+ *Parable of the Ten Women* (Matt. 25:1-13)—"Ballad of the Women" (from *In Love*)

+ *Parable of the Sower* (Luke 8:4-8, 11-15)—"The Sower" (from *Knock, Knock*)

There is also the story of the ingenuous tax collector (Luke 19:1-10), "Zaccheus," *Joy Is Like the Rain;* the transfiguration on Tabor (Mark 9:2-8), "Three Tents," *Knock, Knock;* the Emmaus incident (Luke 24:13-35), "A Long Night," *Seasons;* and so many other biblical moments that lend themselves to song.

+ On feasts of Mary, the celebrant could read these lines from Luke 1:39-46. After announcing, "And Mary said," have the community respond with the Magnificat text (vv. 46-55), in spoken word or in song.

+ At the Christmas liturgy, let the celebrant proclaim Luke 2:1-13. With the announcement of the song of the angels, the congregation continues the Gospel as it sings its "Glory to God" (traditional setting, or the spirited "Song of Glory" from *Gold, Incense and Myrrh*).

Song was the mainstay of oral tradition, the means by which many treasured tales were told, retold, preserved, handed down, integrated, and told again. If we were less pledged to preaching sermons, the child in us could convince us that stories make a

238

better point. Especially story-songs. Rediscover the story of Christmas ("Christmas Ballad," *Gold, Incense and Myrrh*), the story of the one who prepared the way for the Lord ("John," *Knock, Knock*), and listen as little children do, delighted to hear familiar words over and over again, not stifled by repetition, but each time hearing them anew. (All songs and recordings referred to here are by the Medical Mission Sisters.)

Try dramatizing the Easter Gospel.

They often did in medieval times. Use the following program notes or design a drama of your own.

+ In a strong, clear voice, read this opening line: "Early on Sunday morning, while it was still dark, Mary Magdalene went to the tomb" (John 20:1 TEV).

+ Reflect on the Resurrection mystery through Mary Magdalene's liturgical dance.

Use Neil Diamond's "African Trilogy" (from his album *Taproot Manuscript*) as background music, from the threefold *"Christus"* through the thunderclap which, in this context, is perceived as Mary's realization that she has indeed encountered an open, empty tomb.

Identify with Mary as she dances to the mood of the music and the feeling of the feast, moving freely through expressions of fear, disbelief, wonder, joy, ecstasy.

Play close attention to environment. Create a suitable setting through lighting, decor, dress. Add an alabaster jar and, if

239

possible, project a slide of a cave on the back wall to which the dancer can relate. This year, experience the Easter event, not just intellectually, but with the whole of your being: body and mind, soul and spirit.

We have dwelt extensively on how to introduce a community to the notion of shared responsibility for worship (liturgy) and how to prepare them for this through a series of skill-building sessions and various creative stimuli. It is time now for you to give shape to your own ideas and to test them out in practice.

Special Interest Groups

You might begin by forming small standing committees that are related to various aspects of community prayer. Much can be accomplished when those who share like interests work supportively together.

Music (core group)
Visual dimension
Hospitality (welcoming)
Prayers
Movement (gesture, dance)
Drama
Banner-making
Bread-baking
Refreshments
Outreach
  Social action
  Peace and justice
  Mission
Home visiting

The sick
The elderly
The shut-in
Readers (lectors)
Christian educators
  For children
  For youth
  For adults

Resource Room

Set up and maintain a central resource room as a service to worship planners. This center should include reference and sourcebooks, background information, idea books, creative prayer aids, topical files for music and slides, and other helpful material. The following suggestions will help you set up a basic resource room in your community. Add and expand resources as budget permits.

A. *Books*
  General Reference
    The Bible (several translations)
      The Common Bible (Revised Standard Version with Apocrypha)
      The Jerusalem Bible
      The Good News Bible (and others)
    Bible Themes: A Source Book. Vol. 1 and 2. Thierry Maertens. Notre Dame: Fides, 1964.
    The Interpreter's Dictionary of the Bible. Edited by George A. Buttrick. Five volumes. Nashville: Abingdon, 1962–76.
    The Interpreter's One-Volume Commentary on the Bible. Edited by Charles M. Laymon. Nashville: Abingdon, 1971.

Nelson's Complete Concordance (for use with the Revised Standard Version of the Bible) or any concordance that coincides with your preferred translation of the Bible

General Resource

Prayers:

Lord, Be With. Herbert Brokering. St. Louis: Concordia, 1969.

Prayers in Community. Thierry Maertens and Marguerite DeBilde. Notre Dame: Fides, 1974.

Prayers for Everyday Life. Rene Berthier *et al.* Notre Dame: Fides, 1974.

Worship for an Easter People. Frederick A. Styles. Ontario: Enthusia, 1975.

Your Word Is Near. Huub Oosterhuis. New York: Newman, 1968.

Liturgies:

Eucharistic Liturgies. Edited by John Gallen. New York: Newman, 1969.

Home Celebrations. Lawrence E. Moser. New York: Newman, 1970.

Liturgies for Children. Andrew Jamison. St. Anthony Messenger Press, 1975.

Special Effects:

A Time to Dance: Symbolic Movement in Worship. Margaret Fisk Taylor. Philadelphia: United Church Press, 1967.

Banners and Such. Adelaide Ortegel. West Lafayette, Ind.: Center for Contemporary Celebration, 1971.

Creative Dramatics (for children). Mary Paul Francis Pierini. New York: Herder and Herder, 1971.

Light: A Language of Celebration. Kent Schneider

and Adelaide Ortegel. Chicago: Center for Contemporary Celebration, 1973.

There is a vast array of resource books available for contemporary prayer, many of them quite helpful. Spend time in your favorite bookstores and select those that are suited to your situation. Spread the word that a contribution toward the community resource center makes a wonderful gift to the church!

B. *Music*
  Collect and file:
    One copy of every piece of music in use by congregation and choir
    Samples of contemporary music that fulfill criteria for use and may eventually be introduced
    + Published music (songs, hymns, collections)
    + Records and/or cassettes

C. *Slides*
  Set up a central slide collection systematically arranged according to subject and labeled (on slide itself or separately) for proper identification (persons pictured, place, date) and crediting (photographer).
    It is important from the start to design a system for filing slides that allows for quick and easy access and protects against damage.

D. *Other Resources*
  Banners
    Finished banners
    Banner-making materials and ideas
  Candles
    Assorted sizes and shapes for special occasions

243

Recipe(s) for bread-baking
  Leavened
  Unleavened
E. *General Information*
A central bulletin board on which is posted—
  + The community's liturgy (worship) goal and directions
  + The names and phone numbers of leadership team members and the name of the team's contact person
  + The dates, time, and location of the monthly evaluation/planning session
  + A large calendar indicating themes for the Sundays in preparation and the contact person for each
  + Notices pertaining to special interest groups, congregational meetings, community projects
A shelf list of songs and hymns already familiar to the choir and the congregation, thematically arranged. And—
  + A copy of past liturgy (worship) designs
  + Minutes, highlights, points to remember of—
      Leadership team meetings
      Congregational feedback
  + A file of "ideas," sample services, content suggestions for prayer designs, all arranged according to theme

Room Furnishings
  Comfortable chairs, a large table, adequate lighting
  Bookcases and filing cabinets
  Portable stereo and cassette

Light box for slide review
Slide projector and screen
Movie projector

Comments

The resource room can be set up by means of a budget allocation or through gifts from individual donors.

The room should be comfortable and inviting and accessible to all.

There should be periodic "tours" through the resource room to acquaint newcomers with materials and their use.

The community should feel free to use this room during the week to browse, plan, or work at creative projects related to corporate prayer.

It may be beneficial for several smaller churches in an area to pool resources and share a common center.

Summary

We hear God's Word best when we are prepared to hear it, when it is so well presented that it cuts through conditioned apathy with the razor edge of truth, pressing us to respond wholeheartedly by reordering our lives. Sometimes artistic assistance can surprise us out of stereotypes, coax us to listen more closely to what we thought we knew by heart, break us open, lift us up and return us to our roots. Such prayer requires resources, a lot of time, talent, music, in fact, everything we are. It calls for creativity, not to fashion new forms but to enliven existing ones.

Liturgy/Service of the Word	Liturgy/Service of the Eucharist	Liturgy of Life
preparation / presentation / response → (through) → reading, prayer, song, silence, reflection, action → (assisted by) → environment, movement -gesture -ritual action -dance, symbol, drama, visuals		
WORD	*BREAD*	*action*
Hear	**Do**	

Theme: an integrating factor

APPENDIX

SONGS FOR A EUCHARIST OR SERVICE OF WORSHIP

Substitute a theme-of-the-day song for the entrance, offertory, communion, or closing, or use songs appropriate to the liturgical action similar to those suggested here.

"Children of the Lord"— (I John 3:1; Ps. 96:1) — for gathering, focusing, beginning, as we prepare to receive good news

"Take This Bread" (John 14:23; 17:22-23) — for offering ourselves along with Christ who offered himself for us

"Song of Praise" (Matt. 21:9) — a celebrational *Sanctus* in praise of the One who comes in the name of the Lord

"Glory Be!" (Rev. 1:4-6) — an acclamation, the crux of our faith, in a simple song of praise

"Amen!" (Ps. 106:48) — a threefold response to the presence of God; amen, amen, amen!

"God, Our Father" (Matt. 6:9-13) — phrases of the Lord's own prayer strengthen our communion in him

"Be Reconciled!" (II Cor. 5:17-20) — with ourselves, first of all, and with all God's people through the power of our reconciling Lord

247

Take This Bread

Words and music by
Sister Miriam Therese Winter

1. Take this bread,____ take this wine,____ as a prom - ise, as a sign. The life is yours, the love is mine. Let our life and love com - bine.

2. Take this heart.____ It is yours,__ ev'- ry strug - gle it en - dures, all the love it's made to hold, all the warmth, all the cold.

3. Come a - mong ____ us in re - turn.____ In your pres - ence, may we learn that you and I and we are one, and a new life has be - gun.

Song of Praise

Words and music by
Sister Miriam Therese Winter

Ho - ly, Ho - ly, Ho - ly,
come, Lord!____ Ho - ly, Ho - ly, Ho - ly,
come, Lord!____ Ho - ly, Ho - ly, Ho - ly,
come, Lord!____

Verses

1. Lord, your glo - ry fills all cre - a - tion,
2. Come a - gain, O God of the liv - ing,

ev' - ry peo - ple and ev' - ry na - tion.
God of good - ness, faith - ful, for - giv - ing.

All of life pro - claims your praise.
Touch with love our love - less ways.

Glory Be!

Words and music by
Sister Miriam Therese Winter

Glo - ry be to the Fa - ther, and to the Son, and to the Ho - ly Spir - it since the world was be - gun. As it was, and is now, and shall be with-out end. A - men, A - men, A - men.

Amen!

Music by
Sister Miriam Therese Winter

A - men, A - men, A - men!

God, Our Father

Words and music by
Sister Miriam Therese Winter

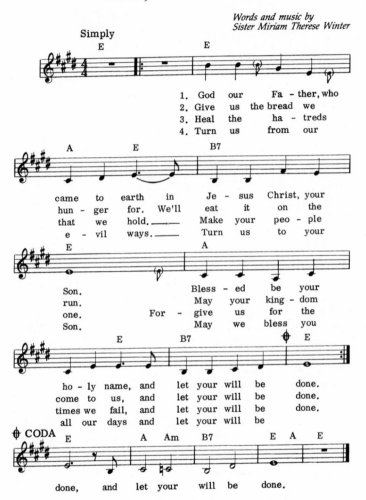

1. God our Fa - ther, who came to earth in Je - sus Christ, your Son. Bless - ed be your ho - ly name, and let your will be done.
2. Give us the bread we hun - ger for. We'll eat it on the run. May your king - dom come to us, and let your will be done.
3. Heal the ha - treds that we hold. Make your peo - ple one. For - give us for the times we fail, and let your will be done.
4. Turn us from our e - vil ways. Turn us to your Son. May we bless you all our days and let your will be

CODA

done, and let your will be done.

Children of the Lord

Words and music by
Sister Miriam Therese Winter

Simply ♩ = 56

1. We are chil-dren of the Lord,_____
2. Fa - ther, hear the song we sing,_____
3. Sing, O chil-dren, to the Lord._____

gath - ered here to pray to - geth - er._____
as we bring our world be - fore you._____
All the world is hushed and wait - ing,_____

_____ We are one with - in His love._____
_____ Soon your Word will sow the seed,_____
_____ as we lift our hearts a - bove,_____

_____ This we know we're cer - tain of.
_____ sow your strength with - in our need.
_____ sim - ply liv - ing in His love.

Be Reconciled!

Key: F Capo 1st Play E

Refrain ♩ = 108

Words and music by
Sister Miriam Therese Winter

NOTES

Chapter One

1. James Carroll, *Contemplation* (Paramus, N. J.: Paulist Press, 1972), pp. 26-27.
2. John Donne, "Batter My Heart."
3. Kenneth Grahame, *The Wind in the Willows*, chap. 7.
4. Ralph Keyes, *We, the Lonely People* (New York: Harper, 1973), p. 10.
5. Laurentius Klein, "Modes of Biblical Faith" (Lecture given at Hope Ecumenical Seminar in Jerusalem, July, 1975).

Chapter Two

1. C. F. D. Moule, *The Birth of the New Testament* (London: A & C Black, 1962), p. 29.
2. Justin Martyr, quoted in *Early Sources of the Liturgy*, ed. Lucien Deiss (New York: Alba House, 1967), p. 25.
3. *Ibid.*, pp. 25-26.
4. Oscar Cullmann, *Early Christian Worship*, trans. by A. S. Todd and J. B. Torrance (London: SCM Press, 1953), p. 33.
5. Alan Watts, *Behold the Spirit* (New York: Vintage Books, 1971), p. 247.
6. Sister Corita, *Footnotes and Headlines* (New York: Herder and Herder and United Church Press, 1967), p. 9.

Chapter Three

1. A chronicler of the Hutterian Brethren, quoted in John Christian Wenger, *Even unto Death* (Richmond: John Knox Press, 1961), p. 113.

2. *Mennonite Encyclopedia,* s.v. "Hymnology of the Anabaptists."

3. Paul M. Miller, "Worship among the Early Anabaptists," *Mennonite Quarterly Review,* 30 (1956), 236.

4. Bishops' Committee on the Liturgy, "The Place of Music in Eucharistic Celebrations," *Newsletter,* January-Feburary, 1968, p. 3.

Chapter Four

1. Rollo May, "Symbols of the Future" (Kansas City: NCR Cassettes, 1974).

2. Paul Tillich, *Theology of Culture* (New York: Oxford University Press, 1964), p. 58.

3. *Ibid.,* p. 59.

4. Dietrich Bonhoeffer, *Letters and Papers from Prison* (New York: Macmillan, 1953), pp. 165-66.

5. Bishops' Committee on the Liturgy, *Music in Catholic Worship* (Washington, DC: U. S. Catholic Conference, 1972), p. 1.

6. Eugene Kennedy, "The Contribution of Religious Ritual to Psychological Balance," *Liturgy in Transition,* vol. 62 of Concilium: Religion in the Seventies, ed. Herman Schmidt, S. J. (New York: Herder and Herder, 1971), p. 53.

7. Maria-Gabriele Wosien, *Sacred Dance: Encounter with the Gods* (New York: Avon Books, 1974), back cover and p. 8.

8. Ambrose of Milan, quoted in Margaret Fisk Taylor, *A Time to Dance* (Philadelphia: United Church Press, 1967), p. 78.

9. Bonaventure, quoted in *ibid.,* p. 90.

10. Kennedy, "Contribution of Religious Ritual," p. 57.

11. Pierre Teilhard de Chardin, *Hymn of the Universe* (New York: Harper, 1961), pp. 26-27.

12. e. e. cummings, "Poem 65."

Chapter Five

1. Gerhard von Rad, *Genesis* (London: SCM Press, 1961), p. 52.

2. Bonhoeffer, *Letters and Papers,* p. 237.

3. Abraham Heschel, quoted in *Intellectual Digest,* June, 1973, pp. 77-78.

4. *Letter to Diognetus,* quoted in *The Apostolic Fathers,* trans. F. X. Glimm *et al.* (Washington: Catholic University of America Press, 1962), pp. 360-61.

5. *Ibid.,* p. 362.

6. Bonhoeffer, *Letters and Papers,* pp. 219-20.

7. Watts, *Behold the Spirit,* p. 246.

8. *The Evening Bulletin* (Philadelphia), January 23, 1977.

9. John H. Yoder, "Exodus and Exile: The Two Faces of Liberation," *Cross Currents,* Fall, 1973, p. 309.